CORE ADV.

Making Sense of
Equations

DR. RANDY PALISOC

IRONBOX®
Education

Copyright © Ironbox Education
This workbook is licensed for **individual classroom or home use only.** Photocopying for an entire school or district is strictly prohibited. To purchase classroom versions at a quantity discount, please visit MathFluency.com.

IRONBOX®
Education

Copyright © Ironbox Education
All rights reserved.

Printed in the United States.

Without limiting the rights under copyright reserved above, no part of this publication may be reproduced, stored in or introduced into a retrieval system, or transmitted, in any form, or by any means (electronic, mechanical, photocopying, recording, or otherwise), without the prior express written permission of the copyright owner.

The scanning, uploading, and distribution of this book via the Internet or via any other means without the permission of the copyright owner is illegal and punishable by law. Please purchase only authorized versions and do not engage in nor encourage electronic piracy of copyrighted materials.

Contents

Essential Background Information

About the Author 4

Making Sense of Equations 5

How does this system work? 5

Pacing 6

Addressing State Learning Standards or the Common Core State Standards 8

Making Sense of Equations

Making Sense of Equations – *Success Tracker* 9

Part 1: The Foundation

Lessons 1-4: One-Step Equations 11

Lessons 5-11: Two-Step Equations 15

Lessons 12-14: Distributive Property and Factoring 22

Lessons 15-17: Order of Operations 25

Lessons 18-21: Substitution 28

Part 2: Applications

Lessons 22-30: Pythagorean Theorem and Its Many Related Skills 32

Lessons 31-32: Absolute Value 41

Lessons: 33-36: Equations Involving Squares and Rectangles 43

Lessons 37-45: Equations Involving Rectangles, Triangles, Parallelograms, and Trapezoids 37

Lessons 46-48: Equations Involving Squares and Circles 66

Lessons 49-51: Equations Involving Three-Dimensional Solids 69

Lessons 52-54: Multi-step Equations 72

Answer Keys and Correcting Student Work 75

About the Author

My name is Dr. Randy Palisoc, and I'm on a mission to give kids **Power Over Numbers** and **Power Over Learning.**

I am a former classroom teacher, and I was a founder of the **five-time national award winning** Synergy Academies, whose elementary school was named the **#1 Urban Elementary School in America** by the National Center for Urban School Transformation in 2013.

The reason I designed this system is that too many students do not have a strong foundation in math, and they do not "get" the standard explanations found in many textbooks. This is troubling because students who struggle early on are often unable catch up to their peers later in life.

On the other hand, students who do have strong foundations have a greater shot at success later in life. In 2013, for example, students who were with Synergy since elementary school (all minority students) had a 95% pass rate on the California High School Exit Exam, compared to only about 79% statewide (all ethnicities).

As shown above, **strong foundations really do matter.**

The Core Advantage math fluency system by Ironbox Education is designed to build those foundations and to build fluency as quickly and as easily as possible. It does so by thinking like kids and teaching in a way that makes sense to them.

I designed this math fluency system based on my experience working with thousands of students from elementary school through high school and finding out what makes them successful. I hope you are able to use this system to give your students or children Power Over Numbers™ and Power Over Learning™!

google "randy palisoc ted talk"

Dr. Randy Palisoc received his Bachelor of Science degree from the University of Southern California (USC), his Master of Education degree from the University of California, Los Angeles (UCLA), and his Doctor of Education degree from USC.

Making Sense of Equations
An Essential Communication Tool for the Language of Math

Whether you realize or not, mathematics is actually a language.

The purpose of a language is to communicate, and mathematics is how we communicate about quantities and logical relationships. We do so by using signs, symbols, and other mathematical terms.

One of the most important communication tools in the language of math is an equation. When students can use equations fluently, it helps them communicate in math more precisely, and it helps them more easily make sense of math.

Equations help us solve a variety of problems, from figuring out how many laps a swimmer must complete during her workout to figuring out how much it will cost to go on vacation.

Like any communication tool, equations are full of nuances. These countless little details can either cause a great deal of confusion, or they can be opportunities to build precision and fluency.

Making Sense of Equations focuses on precision and fluency, and it helps students notice the little details that have a big impact on understanding.

How does this system work?

First things first.

Making Sense of Equations builds precision and fluency, and it requires students to accurately apply the skills that they have learned in previous units. These skills include addition, subtraction, multiplication, division, fractions, integers, and exponents. As you can see, this unit involves many prerequisite skills. Therefore, please make sure students have gone through **all** the prior units before starting this book. **The following units are especially important prerequisites:**

- *10 Powerful Steps to Multiplication Fluency*
- *Making Sense of Fractions*
- *Making Sense of Integers*
- *Making Sense of Exponents*

The Core Advantage series is different from ordinary workbooks. The system is designed to have students work interactively on short, easy-to-understand guided lessons with their teacher or their parent. The reason for this is that when students (especially young students) work with an actual person, it makes learning a much more personal and meaningful experience. **The human touch matters.**

It's important for teachers or parents to watch the lesson-by-lesson demo videos. This way, they'll know the key nuances to point out, and it takes the guesswork and confusion out of the lesson. There are also fully-annotated answer keys that not only show the answer, but also show the steps involved in getting there.

Each lesson provides students with well-thought-out, purposeful practice to promote fluency, and all the lessons build systematically upon each other. The following page provides a suggested pacing plan, and you can adjust the pacing as needed.

Making Sense of Equations | © MathFluency.com | **Teachers: Log in for demo videos.**

Pacing: Making Sense of Equations

Making Sense of Equations involves many prerequisite skills, including addition, subtraction, multiplication, division, fractions, integers, and exponents. Therefore, please make sure students have gone through all of the previous units first. The following units are especially important prerequisites:

- *10 Powerful Steps to Multiplication Fluency*
- *Making Sense of Fractions*
- *Making Sense of Integers*
- *Making Sense of Exponents*

A sample pacing plan for this book is shown on pages 6 and 7, and the pacing can be adjusted as necessary.

	Monday	Tuesday	Wednesday	Thursday	Friday
Week 1	**PART 1 THE FOUNDATION** Lesson 1 One-Step Equations Lesson 2 One-Step Equations	Lesson 3 One-Step Equations Lesson 4 Setting Up and Solving One-Step Equations	Lesson 5 Two-Step Equations Lesson 6 Two-Step Equations	Lesson 7 Two-Step Equations Lesson 8 Two-Step Equations	Lesson 9 Setting Up and Solving Two-Step Equations
Week 2	Lesson 10 Setting Up and Solving Two-Step Equations	Lesson 11 Setting Up and Solving Two-Step Equations Lesson 12 Distributive Property	Lesson 13 Distributive Property Lesson 14 Factoring	Lesson 15 Order of Operations Lesson 16 Order of Operations	Lesson 17 Order of Operations Lesson 18 Substitution
Week 3	Lesson 19 One-Step Equations Lesson 20 Two-Step Equations	Lesson 21 Substitution and Two-Step Equations **PART 2 APPLICATIONS** Lesson 22 Measuring Angles	Lesson 23 Using Properties of Shapes to Find Missing Lengths Lesson 24 Pythagorean Theorem	Lesson 25 Pythagorean Theorem Lesson 26 Squaring Shortcut #1	Lesson 27 Squaring Shortcut #2; Memorizing 11^2 Through 15^2
Week 4	Lesson 28 Pythagorean Theorem	Lesson 29 Approximating Square Roots	Lesson 30 Approximating Square Roots Lesson 31 Absolute Value	Lesson 32 Absolute Value Lesson 33 Geometric Equations	Lesson 34 Difference Between Perimeter and Area of Squares and Rectangles
Week 5	Lesson 35 Perimeter and Area of Squares and Rectangles Lesson 36 Geometric Word Problems	Lesson 37 Difference Between Perimeter and Area of Rectangles and Triangles	Lesson 38 Area of Triangles	Lesson 39 Perimeter and Area of Triangles	Lesson 40 Pythagorean Theorem; Perimeter and Area of Triangles

Pacing (continued)

	Monday	Tuesday	Wednesday	Thursday	Friday
Week 6	Lesson 41 Area of Parallelograms Lesson 42 Perimeter and Area of Parallelograms	Lesson 43 Area of Trapezoids Lesson 44 Trapezoid Equations	Lesson 45 Perimeter and Area of Trapezoids	Lesson 46 Why Pi? Lesson 47 Circumference and Area	Lesson 48 Circumference and Area (Leave Answers in Terms of π)
Week 7	Lesson 49 Volume of Cubes and Rectangular Prisms Lesson 50 Volume of Cubes and Rectangular Prisms	Lesson 51 Volume of Triangular Prisms	Lesson 52 Variables on Both Sides of the Equation	Lesson 53 Variables on Both Sides of the Equation	Lesson 54 Multi-step Equations

Making Sense of Equations | © MathFluency.com | **Teachers: Log in for demo videos.**

Addressing State Learning Standards or the Common Core State Standards

Today, schools across America are either using their own state's learning standards or the Common Core State Standards.

No matter what learning standards a school is using, this system helps give students an academic advantage by building fluency faster than has been possible in the past. Fluency is important for all students because it helps them be more precise, which in turn helps them more easily make sense of math.

Take a look at these two Standards for Mathematical Practice (MP), which are used by states using the Common Core State Standards:

> MP #1: Make sense of problems and persevere in solving them.
> MP #6: Attend to precision.

How do these two math practices go together?

- If students **cannot** attend to precision (#6), then they will not make sense of problems (#1), and they will not persevere in solving them (#1).

On the other hand,

- If students **can** attend to precision (#6), then they are more likely to make sense of problems (#1) and are more likely to persevere in solving them (#1).

As you can see, attending to precision (#6) can mean the difference between confidence and confusion.

The unique Core Advantage system used in this book can help give students an academic advantage in a short amount of time. It is designed to build fluency so that students can attend to precision (#6) and actually understand what they're doing in math.

It does take hard work and practice on the part of students, and only students themselves can determine their level of success based on their effort. The good news is that the greater their level of fluency, the more confidence students will have, and the more likely they are to persevere and put in that necessary hard work and practice.

Fluency matters, and I hope that you are able to use this system to build that fluency with your students.

-- Dr. Randy Palisoc

Name_____

Making Sense of Equations

Part 1 – The Foundation

Go down your **Success Tracker** in the order shown below, and write your score for each of the activities as you complete them. The goal is to make any corrections necessary to earn a score of 100%.

	Lesson	Lesson Name	Score
KEY LESSON	1	One-Step Equations	
	2	One-Step Equations	
	3	One-Step Equations	
KEY LESSON	4	Setting Up and Solving One-Step Equations	
KEY LESSON	5	Two-Step Equations	
	6	Two-Step Equations	
	7	Two-Step Equations	
	8	Two-Step Equations	
KEY LESSON	9	Setting Up and Solving Two-Step Equations	
	10	Setting Up and Solving Two-Step Equations	
	11	Setting Up and Solving Two-Step Equations	
KEY LESSON	12	Distributive Property	
	13	Distributive Property	
KEY LESSON	14	Factoring	
KEY LESSON	15	Order of Operations	
	16	Order of Operations	
	17	Order of Operations	
KEY LESSON	18	Substitution	
	19	One-Step Equations	
	20	Two-Step Equations	
KEY LESSON	21	Substitution and Two-Step Equations	

Name_____

Making Sense of Equations

Part 2 – Applications

Lesson	Lesson Name	Score
22	Measuring Angles	
23	Using Properties of Shapes to Find Missing Lengths	
24	Pythagorean Theorem	
25	Pythagorean Theorem	
26	Squaring Shortcut #1	
27	Squaring Shortcut #2: Memorizing 11^2 Through 15^2	
28	Pythagorean Theorem	
29	Approximating Square Roots	
30	Approximating Square Roots	
31	Absolute Value	
32	Absolute Value	
33	Geometric Equations	
34	Difference Between Perimeter and Area of Squares and Rectangles	
35	Perimeter and Area of Squares and Rectangles	
36	Geometric Word Problems	
37	Difference Between Perimeter and Area of Rectangles and Triangles	
38	Area of Triangles	
39	Perimeter and Area of Triangles	
40	Pythagorean Theorem; Perimeter and Area of Triangles	
41	Area of Parallelograms	
42	Perimeter and Area of Parallelograms	
43	Area of Trapezoids	
44	Trapezoid Equations	
45	Perimeter and Area of Trapezoids	
46	Why Pi?	
47	Circumference and Area	
48	Circumference and Area (Leave Answers in Terms of π)	
49	Volume of Cubes and Rectangular Prisms	
50	Volume of Cubes and Rectangular Prisms	
51	Volume of Triangular Prisms	
52	Extension: Variables on Both Sides of the Equation	
53	Extension: Variables on Both Sides of the Equation	
54	Extension: Multi-step Equations	

KEY LESSON   Name_____

Lesson 1: One-Step Equations

Part 1: Solve.

A.	B. Find the inverse.	C.	D.
5 + 2 = ____	2 ____ ____ = 0	5 · 2 = ____	$\frac{1}{5}$ · ____ = 1
5 − 2 = ____	−4 ____ ____ = 0	5 · −2 = ____	
−5 + 2 = ____	5 ____ ____ = 0	−5 · 2 = ____	**E.**
−5 − 2 = ____	−5 ____ ____ = 0	−5 · −2 = ____	$\frac{5}{\rule{0.5cm}{0.15mm}}$ = 1

Part 2: Solve. Notice and focus on the subtle differences between the problems in each row.

F. $n + 2 = 16$	G. $n - 2 = 16$	H. $2 + n = 16$	I. $2 - n = 16$ Careful! Hidden negative coefficient.
J. $2n = 16$	K. $-2n = 16$	L. $16 = 2n$	M. $16 = -2n$
N. $16 = n + 2$	O. $16 = 2 + n$	P. $16 = n - 2$	Q. $16 = 2 - n$ Careful! Hidden negative coefficient.
R. $\frac{n}{2} = 16$	S. $16 = \frac{n}{2}$	T. $\frac{n}{-5} = 7$	U. $7 = \frac{n}{-6}$

Making Sense of Equations | © MathFluency.com | Teachers: Log in for demo videos.

Lesson 2: One-Step Equations

Part 1: Solve.

A.	B. Find the inverse.	C.	D.
8 + 7 = ____	7 ____ ____ = 0	8 · 7 = ____	$\dfrac{1}{8}$ · ____ = 1
8 − 7 = ____	−9 ____ ____ = 0	8 · −7 = ____	
−8 + 7 = ____	8 ____ ____ = 0	−8 · 7 = ____	**E.**
−8 − 7 = ____	−8 ____ ____ = 0	−8 · −7 = ____	$\dfrac{8}{\_\_\_} = 1$

Part 2: Solve. Notice and focus on the subtle differences between the problems in each row.

F. $a + 3 = -6$	G. $a - 3 = -6$	H. $-3 + a = 6$	I. $3 - a = -6$ Careful! Hidden negative coefficient.
J. $3a = 6$	K. $-3a = -6$	L. $-6 = 3a$	M. $6 = 3a$
N. $-3a = 6$	O. $3a = -6$	P. $-6 = -3a$	Q. $6 = -3a$
R. $\dfrac{a}{-3} = 6$	S. $6 = \dfrac{a}{3}$	T. $\dfrac{a}{6} = -8$	U. $-8 = \dfrac{a}{-7}$

Name_____

Lesson 3: One-Step Equations

Part 1: Solve.

A. 5 + 7 = ____ 5 − 7 = ____ −5 + 7 = ____ −5 − 7 = ____	B. Find the inverse. 7 ____ ____ = 0 −9 ____ ____ = 0 5 ____ ____ = 0 −5 ____ ____ = 0	C. 5 · 7 = ____ 5 · −7 = ____ −5 · 7 = ____ −5 · −7 = ____	D. $\frac{1}{7}$ · ____ = 1 E. $\frac{-7}{}$ = 1

Part 2: Solve. Notice and focus on the subtle differences between the problems in each row.

F. $b + 7 = 42$	G. $b - 7 = 42$	H. $7 + b = -42$	I. $-7 - b = -42$ Careful! Hidden negative coefficient.
J. $7b = 42$	K. $-7b = -42$	L. $-42 = 7b$	M. $42 = 7b$
N. $-7b = 42$	O. $7b = -42$	P. $-42 = -7b$	Q. $42 = -7b$
R. $\frac{b}{7} = 42$	S. $42 = \frac{b}{7}$	T. $\frac{b}{10} = 12$	U. $12 = \frac{b}{11}$

Making Sense of Equations | © MathFluency.com | Teachers: Log in for demo videos. 13

KEY LESSON

Name_____

Lesson 4: Setting Up and Solving One-Step Equations

Directions: Follow along with your instructor to complete this lesson. Set up and solve the equations for the word problems below. Draw a bar model to check your work.

A. A number equals 42. Bar Model:	B. Seven added to a number equals 42. Bar Model:	C. Seven subtracted from a number is 42. Bar Model:
D. A number multiplied by 7 equals 42. Bar Model:	E. A number doubled equals 16. Bar Model:	F. Half of a number equals 16. Bar Model:
G. One third of a number is 21. Bar Model:	H. Two thirds of a number is 8. Bar Model:	I. Three fourths of a number is 15. Bar Model:

14   Making Sense of Equations | © MathFluency.com   **Teachers: Log in for demo videos.**

KEY LESSON

Name_____

Lesson 5: Two-Step Equations

Part 1: Solve.

A.	B. Find the inverse.	C.	D.
3 + 6 = ____	6 ____ ____ = 0	3 · 6 = ____	$\frac{1}{6}$ · ____ = 1
3 − 6 = ____	−8 ____ ____ = 0	3 · −6 = ____	
−3 + 6 = ____	3 ____ ____ = 0	−3 · 6 = ____	E.
−3 − 6 = ____	−3 ____ ____ = 0	−3 · −6 = ____	$\frac{-6}{\_\_\_\_}$ = 1

Part 2: Solve. Notice and focus on the subtle differences between the problems in each row.

F. $3n + 6 = 21$	G. $3n - 6 = 21$	H. $-3n + 6 = 21$ Be careful!	I. $-3n - 6 = 21$
J. $6 - 3n = 21$ Be careful!	K. $6 + 3n = 21$	L. $-6 - 3n = 21$	M. $-6 + 3n = 21$
N. $21 = 3n + 6$	O. $21 = -3n + 6$	P. $21 = 3n - 6$	Q. $21 = -3n - 6$
R. $21 = -6 - 3n$	S. $21 = 6 + 3n$	T. $21 = -6 + 3n$	U. $21 = 6 - 3n$

Lesson 6: Two-Step Equations

Part 1: Solve.

A.	B. Find the inverse.	C.	D.
4 + 3 = ____	3 ____ ____ = 0	3 · 3 = ____	$\dfrac{1}{4}$ · ____ = 1
4 − 3 = ____	−5 ____ ____ = 0	3 · −3 = ____	
−4 + 3 = ____	4 ____ ____ = 0	−4 · 3 = ____	E.
−4 − 3 = ____	−4 ____ ____ = 0	−4 · −3 = ____	$\dfrac{-4}{\_\_\_\_}$ = 1

Part 2: Solve. Notice and focus on the subtle differences between the problems in each row.

F. **NEW TYPE OF PROBLEM** $3(y+2)=18$	G. $-3(y-2)=18$	H. $-3(y+2)=-18$	I. $-3(y-2)=-18$
J. $9-3y=-6$	K. $9+3y=-6$	L. $-9-3y=-6$	M. $-9+3y=-6$
N. $-6=2(y+9)$	O. $-6=-2(y+9)$	P. $-6=2(y-9)$	Q. $-6=-2(y-9)$
R. $-6=-9-3y$	S. $-6=9+3y$	T. $-6=-9+3y$	U. $-6=9-3y$

Name_____

Lesson 7: Two-Step Equations

Part 1: Solve.

A.	B. Find the inverse.	C.	D.
$7 + 4 =$ ___	4 ___ ___ $= 0$	$7 \cdot 4 =$ ___	$\dfrac{1}{7} \cdot$ ___ $= 1$
$7 - 4 =$ ___	-6 ___ ___ $= 0$	$7 \cdot -4 =$ ___	
$-7 + 4 =$ ___	7 ___ ___ $= 0$	$-7 \cdot 4 =$ ___	E.
$-7 - 4 =$ ___	-7 ___ ___ $= 0$	$-7 \cdot -4 =$ ___	$\dfrac{7}{\text{___}} = 1$

Part 2: Solve. Notice and focus on the subtle differences between the problems in each row.

F. ⬦ NEW TYPE OF PROBLEM $\dfrac{a}{4} + 6 = 12$	G. $\dfrac{a}{3} - 6 = 12$	H. $\dfrac{a}{6} + 7 = 12$	I. $\dfrac{a}{6} - 7 = 12$
J. $-8 + \dfrac{a}{5} = 12$	K. $-8 - \dfrac{a}{5} = 12$	L. $8 + \dfrac{a}{6} = 12$	M. $8 - \dfrac{a}{6} = 12$
N. $12 = \dfrac{a}{5} + 7$	O. $12 = -3 + \dfrac{a}{7}$	P. $12 = 7 - \dfrac{a}{3}$	Q. $12 = \dfrac{a}{5} - 6$
R. $\dfrac{5}{7}a + 2 = 12$	S. $\dfrac{3}{5}a - 6 = 12$	T. $\dfrac{2}{3}a + 6 = 12$	U. $\dfrac{4}{5}a - 8 = 12$

Making Sense of Equations | © MathFluency.com | **Teachers: Log in for demo videos.**

Name_____

Lesson 8: Two-Step Equations

Part 1: Solve.

A.	B. Find the inverse.	C.	D.
2 + 6 = ___	6 ___ ___ = 0	2 · 6 = ___	$\frac{1}{6}$ · ___ = 1
2 − 6 = ___	−8 ___ ___ = 0	2 · −6 = ___	
−2 + 6 = ___	2 ___ ___ = 0	−2 · 6 = ___	E.
−2 − 6 = ___	−2 ___ ___ = 0	−2 · −6 = ___	$\frac{-6}{\underline{}} = 1$

Part 2: Solve. Notice and focus on the subtle differences between the problems in each row.

F. **NEW TYPE OF PROBLEM** $\frac{b+9}{4} = -5$	G. $\frac{b-9}{3} = -5$	H. $\frac{b+9}{6} = 5$	I. $\frac{b-9}{6} = -5$
J. $-8 + \frac{b}{5} = -5$	K. $8 + \frac{b}{5} = -5$	L. $-8 + \frac{b}{6} = -5$	M. $8 + \frac{b}{6} = -5$
N. $-5 = \frac{b+7}{5}$	O. $-5 = \frac{b-3}{7}$	P. $5 = \frac{b+7}{3}$	Q. $-5 = \frac{b-7}{5}$
R. $3 - \frac{4}{5}b = -5$	S. $-7 + \frac{2}{3}b = -5$	T. $-5 + \frac{2}{3}b = -5$	U. $7 - \frac{2}{3}b = -5$

KEY LESSON

Name_____

Lesson 9: Setting Up and Solving Two-Step Equations

Part 1: Follow along with your instructor to complete this lesson. Set up and solve the equations for the word problems below. Draw a bar model to check your work.

A. Six added to three times a number is 21. Bar Model:	B. Six subtracted from three times a number is 21. Bar Model:
C. Eight subtracted from one fourth of a number is 12. Bar Model:	D. Seven added to one fourth of a number is 12. Bar Model:

Part 2: Set up and solve the equations for the word problems below.

E. Three times a number <u>subtracted from 6</u> is 21.	F. Three times a number subtracted from 6 is −21.

Making Sense of Equations | © MathFluency.com | **Teachers: Log in for demo videos.**

KEY LESSON

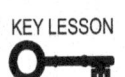

Name_____

Lesson 10: Setting Up and Solving Two-Step Equations

Directions: Set up and solve each equation. Both problems in each row are the same type of problem.

A. A gym charges $25 a month for membership. In addition to the monthly fee, it charges $7 for each dance class. Sara spent $81 in one month. How many dance classes did she attend?	B. Admission to a football game was $27. In addition, every menu item at the concession stand was $4. A fan spent $43 for admission and for food and beverages. How many items did he buy at the concession stand?
C. A hotel charges $180 a night for a room. In addition to the nightly rate, it charges a resort fee for each night of the visit. A family spent four nights at the hotel, and their bill was $800. How much was the resort fee each night?	D. A driver rented a car for $40 a day. In addition, he purchased accident insurance for each day of the rental. The total bill for a 7-day rental was $371. How much did accident insurance cost each day?
E. A clothing store sold half of its shirts on Monday. The next morning, it received a shipment of 24 new shirts. Now it has 54 shirts in stock. How many shirts did it have originally?	F. A student read one third of a book after school. Later that evening, he read 7 more pages. He has now read 22 pages in all. How many pages does the book have?
G. A restaurant has some potatoes in its kitchen, and it bought 24 more to get ready for dinner. It then used half of all its potatoes that night, leaving it with only 16. What was the original number of potatoes in the restaurant?	H. A store had some books on a shelf, and it removed 5 of them. Later, it sold 1/3 of the books that were on the shelf, leaving 2/3 of the books unsold. Now there are 18 books left on the shelf. How many books were originally on the shelf?

20   Making Sense of Equations | © MathFluency.com | **Teachers:** Log in for demo videos.

Name_____

Lesson 11: Setting Up and Solving Two-Step Equations

Directions: Set up and solve each equation. Both problems in each row are the same type of problem.

A. Jennifer started her trip with $84. She bought 3 bottles of water, and now she has $72.75 left. How much did each bottle of water cost?	B. To rent a bike at the beach, it costs $15 upfront, plus an additional $7 per hour. How many hours was a bike rented if the total cost was $36?
C. A plane ticket costs $220. In addition to the airfare, each passenger must pay a landing fee. A family of three paid $714. How much is the landing fee per passenger?	D. Every book ordered from an online store costs $12. In addition, the customer pays a shipping charge for every book. A customer purchases 5 books, spending $80. How much is the shipping charge for each book?
E. An airplane completed three fifths of its flight before noon. A short while later, it traveled an additional 125 miles, for a total of 1,625 miles. How many miles long was the total flight?	F. A bird ate 3/4 of the food in her dish, leaving only 1/4 of her food in the dish. Later, her owner added 17 grams of food to the dish, bringing the total to 26 grams. What was the original amount of food in the dish?
G. John started with $21. Then, he received some money for his allowance. Later, he spent 2/3 of all his money on a toy, leaving him with 1/3 of his money. Now he has $9. How much did he receive for his allowance?	H. A cooler had 42 cups of water in it. A team's coach added another 16 cups. The team then drank half of the water in the cooler. How much water was left in the cooler?

KEY LESSON

Name_____

Lesson 12: Distributive Property

Part 1: Follow along with your instructor to complete this lesson.

A. Multiply.	B. Expand vertically.	C. Expand vertically, then multiply.
3 2 1 × 3	3 2 1	3 2 1 × 3 3 × 1 3 × 20 3 × 300 Sum

D. Expand horizontally. 321 =	E. Expand horizontally, then multiply 3(321) =

Part 2: Multiply. Notice and focus on the subtle differences between the problems in each set.

F. $2(a + 4)$	G. $2(a - 4)$	H. $2(-a + 4)$	I. $2(-a - 4)$
J. $-2(a + 4)$	K. $-2(a - 4)$	L. $-2(-a + 4)$	M. $-2(-a - 4)$
N. $3(b + 5)$	O. $-5(-c + 8)$	P. $-4(d - 3)$	Q. $-1(-e - 9)$
R. $-(-f - 3)$	S. $-(g - 2)$	T. $-(-h + 7)$	U. $-(k + 3)$

Name_____

Lesson 13: Distributive Property

Part 1: Use the distributive property to multiply. Write your negative signs clearly.

A. $a(b + c)$	B. $a(-b + c)$	C. $-a(b + c)$	D. $-a(-b + c)$
E. $a(b - c)$	F. $a(-b - c)$	G. $-a(b - c)$	H. $-a(-b - c)$

Part 2: Use the distributive property to multiply. Write your negative signs clearly.

I. $2(3a + 1)$	J. $-3(-5e - 8)$	K. $-3a(2a - 3b + c)$
L. $-1(-5b + 4)$	M. $-(3a - c + 6)$	N. $-5a(2a - 5b - 2c)$
O. $-5(6c - 5)$	P. $8(-6g + 3)$	Q. $-a(-9a^2 - 3a)$
R. $-(-9d^2 - 2d)$	S. $-6h(3h^2 + 7h)$	T. $-5a(-6a^3 - 2a^2 + a)$

Making Sense of Equations | © MathFluency.com | Teachers: Log in for demo videos.

KEY LESSON

Name_____

Lesson 14: Factoring

Part 1: Simplify using the GCF (Greatest Common <u>Factor</u>). Remember to ask the Magic Question first.

A. $\dfrac{8}{10}$	B. $\dfrac{10}{25}$	C. $\dfrac{5}{25}$	D. $\dfrac{6}{21}$	E. $\dfrac{4}{16}$
F. $\dfrac{12}{16}$	G. $\dfrac{18}{30}$	H. $\dfrac{12}{12}$	I. $\dfrac{3}{15}$	J. $\dfrac{20}{20}$

Part 2: Factor each expression. Then, multiply the factors to check your work.

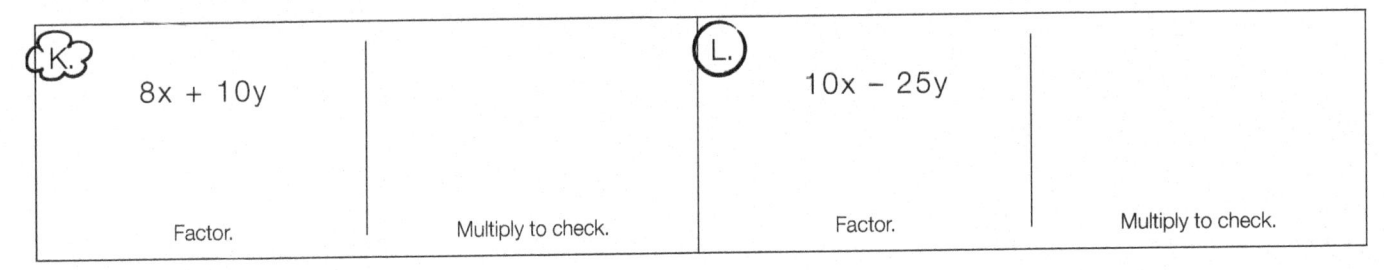

K. $8x + 10y$		L. $10x - 25y$	
Factor.	Multiply to check.	Factor.	Multiply to check.

Part 3: Factor each expression.

M. $5a + 25b$	N. $3c + 15d$	O. $12e + 16f$	P. $20x + 20y + 20z$
Q. $4m - 16n$	R. $-12r - 12s$	S. $-6t - 9u$	T. $18v - 30w$
Careful! Negative values.	Hint: Factor out −12.	Hint: Factor out a negative value.	

Part 4: Follow along with your instructor to factor each expression. Use the extra white space as scratch paper.

U. $7a + 49ab$	V. $10x - 25xy$	W. $8c^2 - 64c$	X. $9x^3 + 81x^2$

Making Sense of Equations | © MathFluency.com | **Teachers: Log in for demo videos.**

KEY LESSON

Name_____

Lesson 15: Order of Operations

Part 1: Follow along with your instructor to complete this lesson.

The expressions in Box A and Box B use the same numbers of ____, ____, and ____. They also use the same operations of _____ and _____. The _____ tell us which operation to perform first.

- In Box A, the parentheses tell us to perform the _____ operation first.
- In Box B, the parentheses tell us to perform the _____ operation first.

A. $(2 + 5) \times 3$	B. $2 + (5 \times 3)$

Even though Box A and Box B used the same numbers and the same operations, they each gave us different _____. This shows that the order of operations _____. To prevent _____ and to make sure everyone gets the same value when simplifying expressions and equations, we use the following _____ ____ _____.

- First, perform the operations inside the _____ or other grouping symbols.
- Then, simplify _____ and roots.
- Next, simplify both _____ and _____ from left to right.
- Finally, simplify both _____ and _____ from left to right.

Use the common acronym ____ ____ ____ ____ ____ ____ to remember the order of operations.

Part 2: Simplify each expression using the order of operations.

C. $4 + 3^2$	D. $(4 + 3)^2$

Name_____

Lesson 16: Order of Operations

Part 1: Simplify each expression using the order of operations (P E MD AS).

A. $6 + 3 \times 4 \div 2 - 1$	B. $6 + 3 \times 4 \div (2 - 1)$
C. $(6 + 3 \times 4) \div 2 - 1$	D. $6 + 3 \times (4 \div 2 - 1)$

Part 2: This next set of problems uses only multiplication, division, addition, and subtraction. Remember that **multiplication and division** take precedence over **addition and subtraction**. To make this easier to see, use parentheses to group together numbers that are being multiplied or divided. Then, simplify.

Example: $5 + 6 \div 2 + 3 \times 4 \div 2$
  $= 5 + (6 \div 2) + (3 \times 4 \div 2)$
  $= 5 + 3 + 6$
  $= 14$

E. $8 \div 2 + 9 \div 3 \times 2 - 10$	F. $3 + 5 \times 3 - 10 \div 2 \times 3$
G. $4 \times 5 - 6 \times 3 + 8 \div 4$	H. $9 - 14 \div 2 + 4 + 5 \times 2$
I. $8 - 4 \div 2 + 6 + 2 \times 4$	J. $5 - 9 \div 3 + 12 \div 6 \times 2$

Lesson 17: Order of Operations

Part 1: Simplify each expression using the order of operations (P E MD AS). Some of these problems involve exponents and nested parentheses (parentheses within parentheses).

A. $(2)(3)(4)$	B. $2^2(12 \div (3 + 1))$
C. $\dfrac{20}{((4^2 + 3^2) \div 5) - 1}$	D. $\dfrac{(5 + 1)^2 + (6 + 2)^2}{10^2}$

Part 2: Simplify each expression using the order of operations. These answers will involve fractions and negative values. **Use parentheses** to show that multiplication and division take precedence over addition and subtraction.

E. $1 \div 10 + 3 \div 10 + 5 \div 10$	F. $10 \div 1 \times 3 \div 6 - 2 \times 4$
G. $6 - 12 \div 6 \times 2 - 10 + 1$	H. $1 + 2 \times 3 \div 7 + 4 \times 5$
I. $3 - 10 \div 5 \times 9 \div 6 - 8$	J. $2 \div 5 + 1 \div 5 + 7 \times 2$

Lesson 18: Substitution

Part 1: Substitute, then simplify. **x = 3, y = 4**

A. x + y	B. x − y	C. −x + y	D. −x − y

Part 2: Substitute, then simplify. Notice and focus on the subtle differences between the problems in each row.

E. $a = 2, b = 7$ $3a + b$	F. $a = 3, b = 8$ $3a - b$	G. $a = 5, b = 2$ $-3a + b$	H. $a = 2, b = 3$ $-3a - b$
I. $c = (-10), d = 2$ $c + 4d$	J. $c = 15, d = 1$ $c - 4d$	K. $c = 8, d = 2$ $-c + 4d$	L. $c = 3, d = 1$ $-c - 4d$
M. $e = 2, f = 3$ $3ef + 2e$	N. $e = 4, f = 2$ $3ef - 2e$	O. $e = 5, f = 1$ $-3ef + 2e$	P. $e = 8, f = 0$ $-3ef - 2e$
Q. $g = (-4), h = 5$ $g + gh$	R. $g = (-5), h = (-10)$ $g - gh$	S. $g = 2, h = 3$ $-g + gh$	T. $g = 5, h = 3$ $-g - gh$

Name_____

Lesson 19: One-Step Equations

Part 1: Subtract. For Box C and Box D, use either **Stepping Stones** or the shortcut for subtracting with zeroes.

A.	B.	C.	D.
25 − 16	225 − 81	100 − 64	400 − 256

Part 2: Solve for x, a^2, b^2, or c^2. Notice the similarities between Box E in Row 1 and Box I in Row 2.

E. $x + 16 = 25$	F. $36 + x = 100$	G. $25 + 144 = x$	H. $81 + 1600 = x$
I. $a^2 + 16 = 25$	J. $a^2 + 144 = 169$	K. $a^2 + 64 = 100$	L. $a^2 + 256 = 400$
M. $81 + b^2 = 225$	N. $100 + b^2 = 676$	O. $64 + b^2 = 289$	P. $49 + b^2 = 625$
Q. $225 + 400 = c^2$	R. $81 + 144 = c^2$	S. $144 + 256 = c^2$	T. $81 + 1600 = c^2$

Making Sense of Equations | © MathFluency.com | **Teachers: Log in for demo videos.**

Name_____

Lesson 20: Two-Step Equations

Part 1: Evaluate the Squares.

A. 1^2	B. 2^2	C. 3^2	D. 4^2	E. 5^2
F. 6^2	G. 7^2	H. 8^2	I. 9^2	J. 10^2

Part 2: Find the square roots (write only the positive root).

K. $\sqrt{9}$	L. $\sqrt{36}$	M. $\sqrt{25}$	N. $\sqrt{81}$	O. $\sqrt{100}$
P. $\sqrt{a^2}$	Q. $\sqrt{b^2}$	R. $\sqrt{c^2}$	S. $\sqrt{x^2}$	T. $\sqrt{y^2}$

Part 3: Solve for a, b, or c.

Example: $a^2 + 16 = 25$	U. $a^2 + 64 = 100$	V. $a^2 + 144 = 225$	W. $a^2 + 144 = 169$
X. $9 + b^2 = 25$	Y. $36 + b^2 = 100$	Z. $a^2 + 225 = 289$	AA. $a^2 + 1600 = 1681$
AB. $a^2 + 576 = 676$	AC. $a^2 + 576 = 625$	AD. $9 + 16 = c^2$	AE. $36 + 64 = c^2$

Making Sense of Equations | © MathFluency.com | **Teachers: Log in for demo videos.**

KEY LESSON

Name_____

Lesson 21: Substitution and Two-Step Equations

Part 1: Substitute and evaluate.

A. $a = 3$ $a^2 =$	B. $a = 6$ $a^2 =$	C. $b = 4$ $b^2 =$	D. $b = 8$ $b^2 =$
E. $b = 12$ $b^2 =$	F. $b = 24$ $b^2 =$	G. $c = 13$ $c^2 =$	H. $c = 25$ $c^2 =$

Part 2: Find the square roots (write only the positive root).

I. $\sqrt{9}$	J. $\sqrt{36}$	K. $\sqrt{25}$	L. $\sqrt{81}$
M. $\sqrt{a^2}$	N. $\sqrt{b^2}$	O. $\sqrt{c^2}$	P. $\sqrt{x^2}$

Part 3: Substitute, then solve for the unknown variable (a, b, or c).

Q. Solve for a. $b = 4, c = 5$ $a^2 + b^2 = c^2$	R. Solve for b. $a = 6, c = 10$ $a^2 + b^2 = c^2$	S. Solve for a. $b = 12, c = 13$ $a^2 + b^2 = c^2$	T. Solve for a. $b = 24, c = 25$ $a^2 + b^2 = c^2$
U. Solve for c. $a = 3, b = 4$ $a^2 + b^2 = c^2$	V. Solve for c. $a = 6, b = 8$ $a^2 + b^2 = c^2$	W. Solve for a. $b = 8, c = 10$ $a^2 + b^2 = c^2$	X. Solve for b. $a = 3, c = 5$ $a^2 + b^2 = c^2$

Making Sense of Equations | © MathFluency.com | **Teachers: Log in for demo videos.**

Name_____

Lesson 22: Measuring Angles

Part 1: Angles – Measure each angle. Then, find the right angle, corner it, and label it **"right angle."**

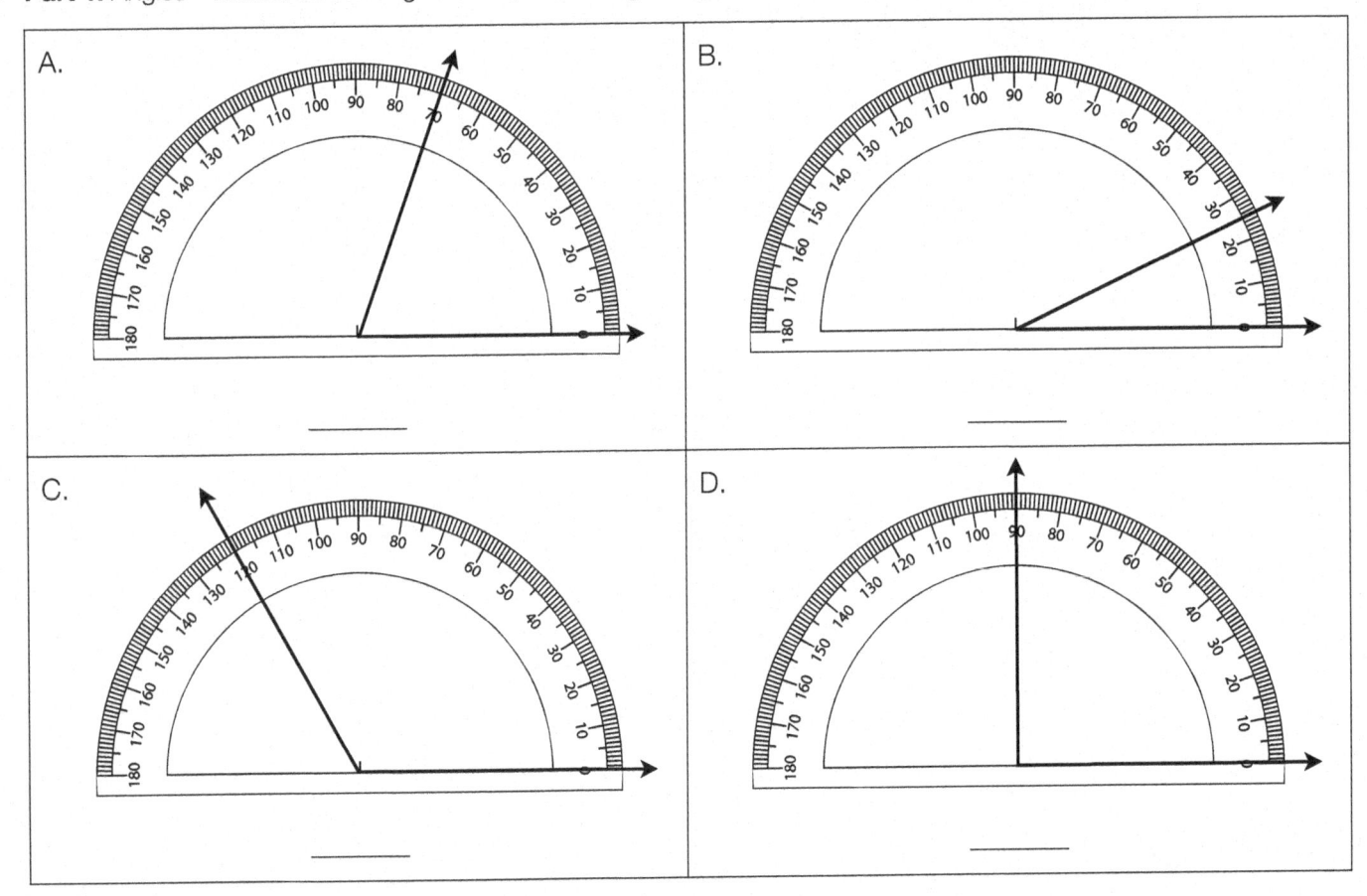

A.

B.

C.

D.

Part 2: Look for the right angles and write **"90°"** and the words **"right angle"** next to them. For the other angles, indicate whether they measure **< 90°** or **> 90°**.

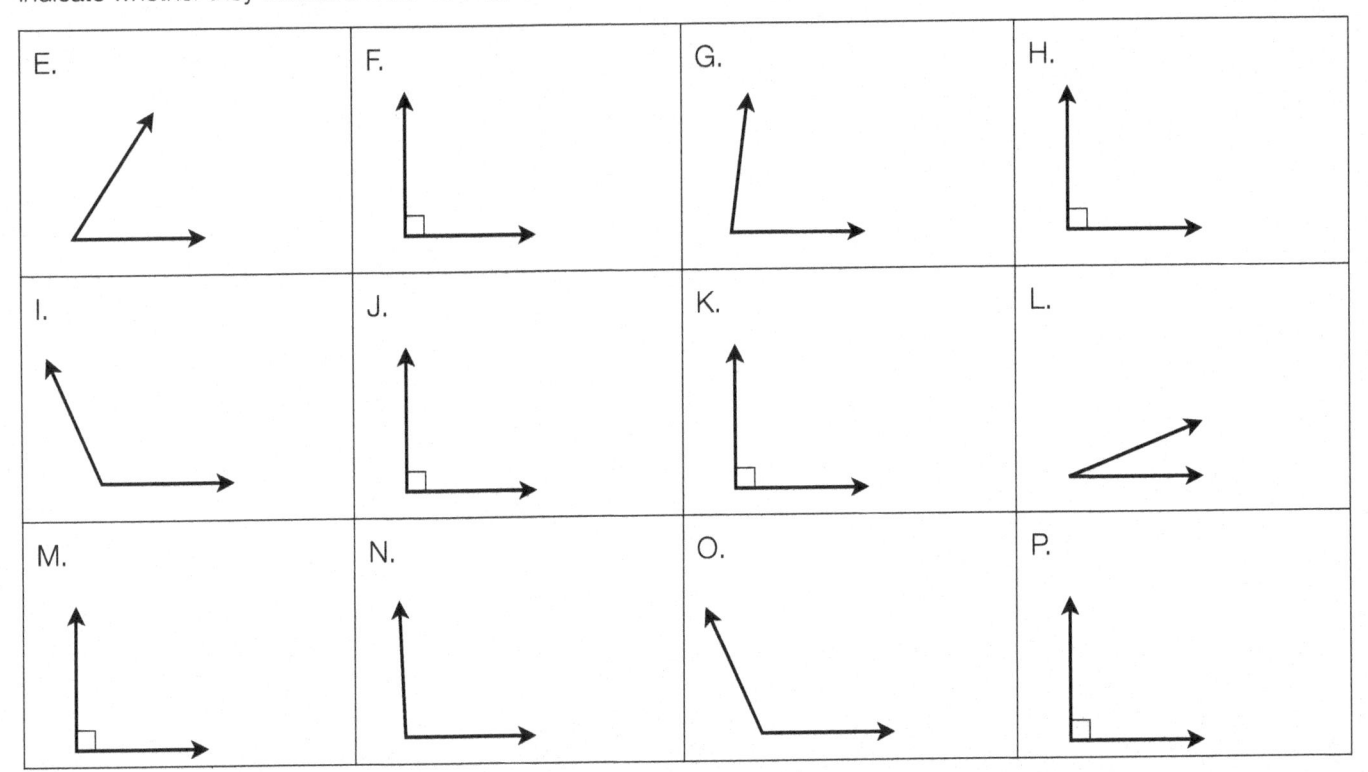

E.

F.

G.

H.

I.

J.

K.

L.

M.

N.

O.

P.

32 Making Sense of Equations | © MathFluency.com | **Teachers: Log in for demo videos.**

KEY LESSON

Name_____

Lesson 23: Using Properties of Shapes to Find Missing Lengths

Directions: Follow along with your instructor. Use properties to identify the shapes and to find the lengths of the missing sides. If there is not enough information, write, **"Not enough info."** Use the shape names below:

square	equilateral triangle	
rectangle	isosceles triangle	isosceles right triangle
	scalene triangle	scalene right triangle

A. _____

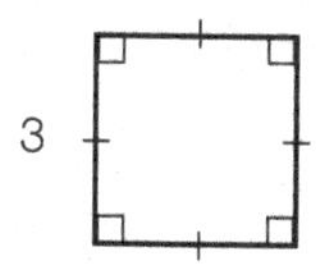

3

B. _____

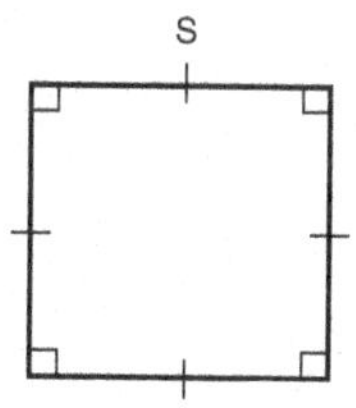

s

C. _____

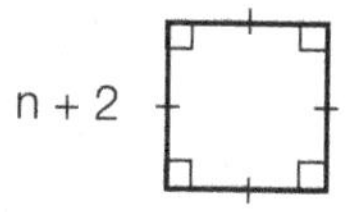

n + 2

D. _____

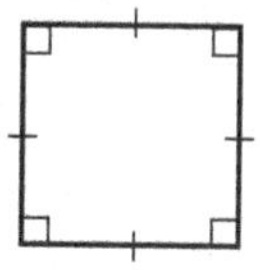

E. _____

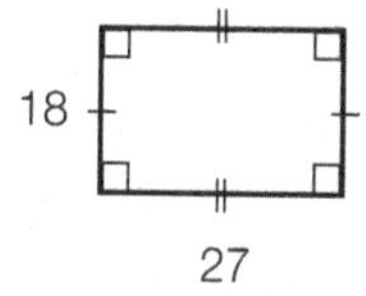

18
27

F. _____

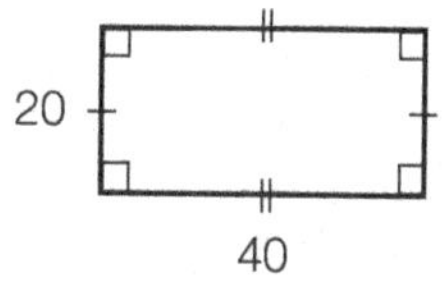

20
40

G. _____

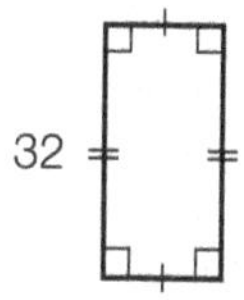

32

H. _____

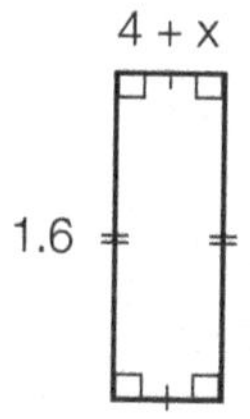

4 + x
1.6

I. _____

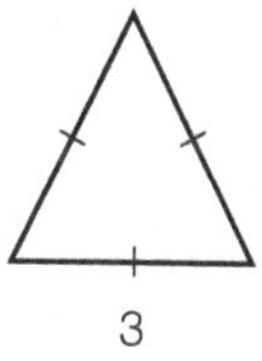

3

J. _____

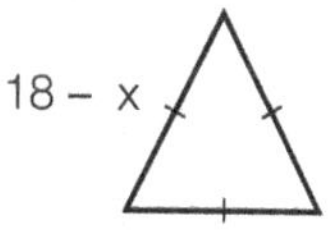

18 − x

K. _____

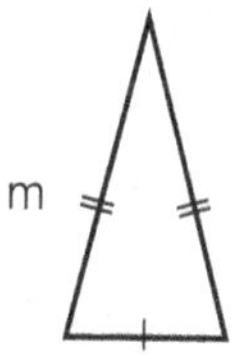

m

L. _____

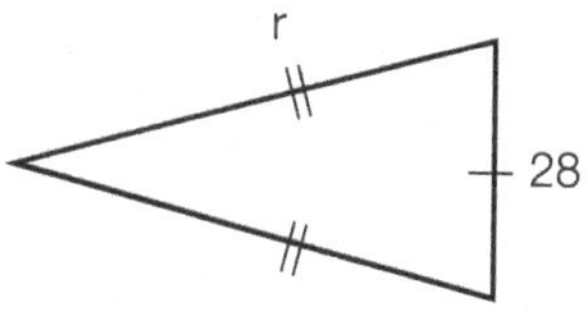

r
28

M. _____

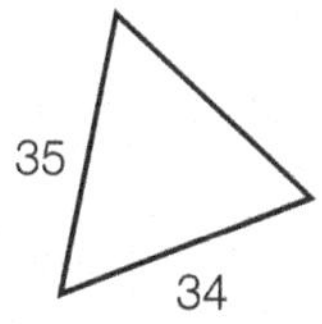

35
34

N. _____

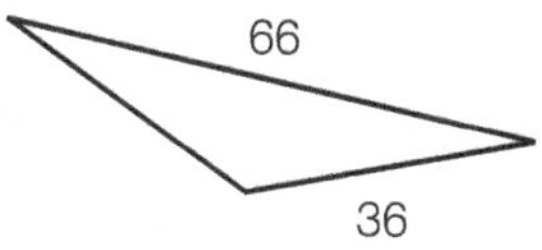

66
36

O. _____

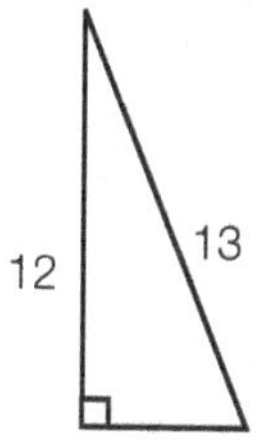

12, 13

P. _____

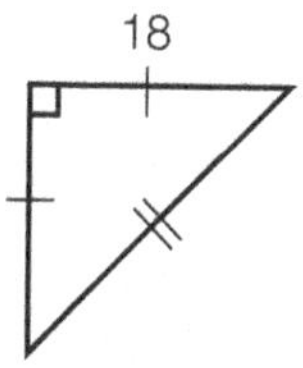

18

Making Sense of Equations | © MathFluency.com | Teachers: Log in for demo videos.

KEY LESSON

Name_____

Lesson 24: Pythagorean Theorem

Part 1: Find the two right triangles and label them *"right triangle."* Then, label the right angles *"90°."*

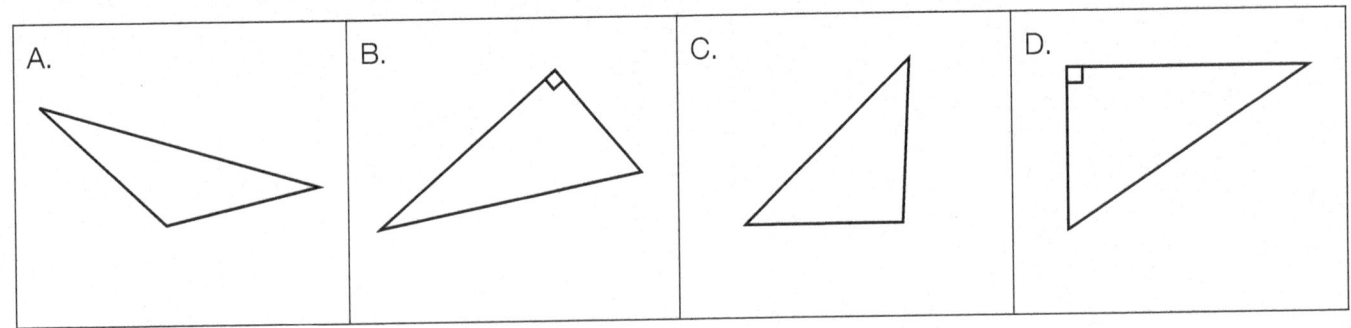

A.	B.	C.	D.

Part 2: Find the lengths of the missing sides. If there is not enough information, write *"Not enough info."*

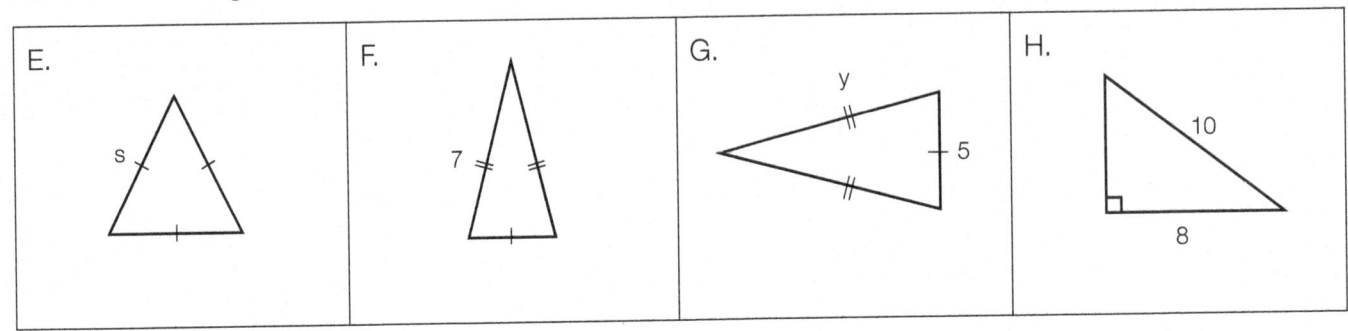

E.	F.	G.	H.
s	7	y, 5	10, 8

Part 3: Follow along with your instructor to learn about the Pythagorean Theorem. **Little Secret:** You've already learned how to use the Pythagorean Theorem in Lessons 19, 20, 21, 22, and 23.

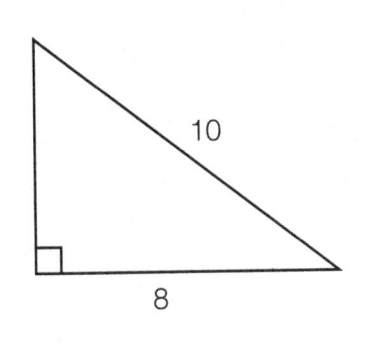

Step 1	Make sure you are working with a _____ _____.
Step 2	Label the sides ____, ____, and ____. Side ____ is called the _____. It is the _____ side and is _____ from the _____ _____. It does not _____ the right angle.
Step 3	Solve using the formula ____ + ____ = ____ (just like Lesson 20)

Use the Pythagorean Theorem to find the length of the missing side. Use the workspace to the right.

(Triangle with legs 8 and hypotenuse 10)

34   Making Sense of Equations | © MathFluency.com | **Teachers:** Log in for demo videos.

Name_____

Lesson 25: Pythagorean Theorem

Part 1: Solve. For Box C and Box D, use either **Stepping Stones** or the shortcut for subtracting with zeroes.

A.	B.	C.	D.	E.
1 2 x 1 2	1 5 x 1 5	1 0 0 − 6 4	1 0 0 − 3 6	2 2 5 − 1 4 4

Part 2: Solve using the Pythagorean Theorem ($a^2 + b^2 = c^2$). Label sides a, b, and c first (a = shortest, c = longest). Be careful since the right angle changes positions from problem to problem. If a triangle is not a right triangle, cross it out and write, *"Not a right triangle."*

F. (right triangle: legs 4 and 5)

G. (right triangle: legs 8 and 10)

H. (triangle: sides 26 and 24)

I. (right triangle: sides 5 and 3)

J. (right triangle: sides 10 and 6)

K. (right triangle: sides 15 and 12)

L. (right triangle: sides 4 and 3)

M. (right triangle: sides 8 and 6)

KEY LESSON

Lesson 26: Squaring Shortcut #1

Name_____

Part 1: Multiply using the standard algorithm.

A.	B.	C.	D.
2 5 x 2 5	3 5 x 3 5	4 5 x 4 5	5 5 x 5 5

Part 2: Follow along with your instructor to learn Squaring Shortcut #1. **This shortcut is very elegant, but it only works when squaring a base that ends with the number 5.**

E.	F.	G.	H.
2 5 x 2 5	3 5 x 3 5	4 5 x 4 5	5 5 x 5 5

Part 3: Follow along with your instructor to learn why Squaring Shortcut #1 works. Box I involves using expanded notation in the workspace. Box J involves factoring (refer to Lesson 14, Box P for a hint).

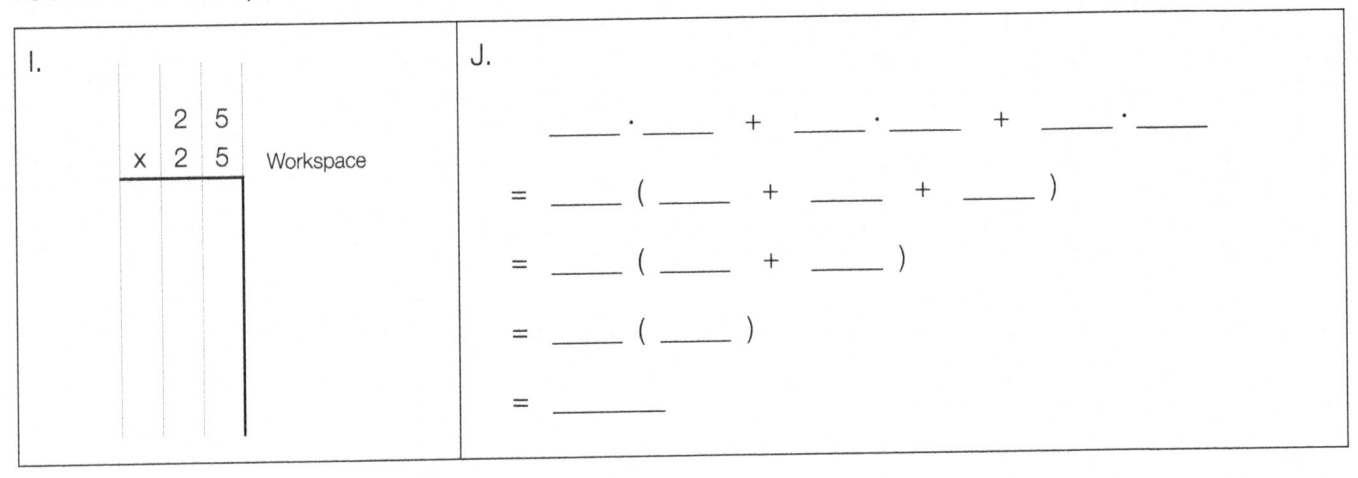

I.
  2 5
x 2 5   Workspace

J.
____ · ____ + ____ · ____ + ____ · ____

= ____ (____ + ____ + ____)

= ____ (____ + ____)

= ____ (____)

= ____

Part 4: Use the squaring shortcut that you just learned for bases that end with the number 5.

K.
  1 5
x 1 5

L.
  1 0 5
x 1 0 5

HINT:
5 x 5 = 25. Next, cross off "10" and write "11." Use the hanging zero shortcut to multiply 11 x 10.

M.
65 x 65 = _____

75 x 75 = _____

85 x 85 = _____

95 x 95 = _____

N.
35^2 = _____

25^2 = _____

45^2 = _____

15^2 = _____

36 Making Sense of Equations | © MathFluency.com | **Teachers: Log in for demo videos.**

Name_____

Lesson 27: Squaring Shortcut #2; Memorizing 11^2 Through 15^2

The next lesson (Lesson 28) will be much easier if you can memorize the following: 11^2, 12^2, 13^2, 14^2, and 15^2.

Since the number 15 ends with a "5," you can easily figure out 15^2 by using the very elegant Squaring Shortcut #1. The numbers 11, 12, 13, and 14 do not end with a "5," so you can't use Squaring Shortcut #1. However, there is a different shortcut that you can use to help you memorize their squares, **although it's not nearly as elegant.**

Use this shortcut only for squaring two-digit numbers that begin with "1" (the numbers 11-19).

Part 1: Follow along with your instructor to complete this lesson.

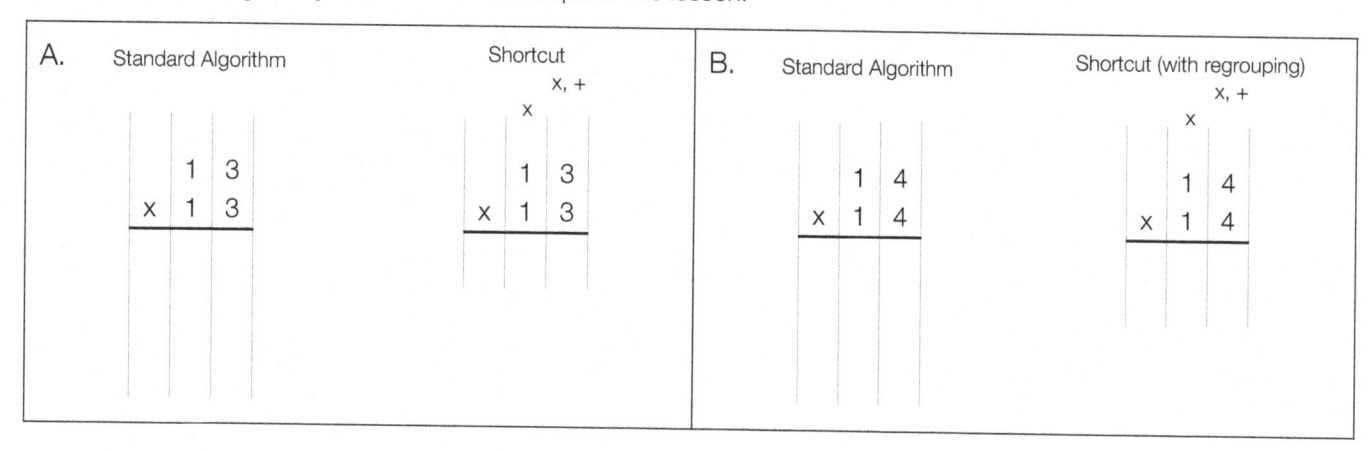

A. Standard Algorithm   Shortcut
     13   13
   × 13   × 13

B. Standard Algorithm   Shortcut (with regrouping)
     14   14
   × 14   × 14

Part 2: Use the squaring shortcut.

C.   D.   E.   F.
   12   11   19   17
 × 12   × 11   × 19   × 17

Part 3: Work on one column at a time to **memorize** the squares shown below.

- First, study the problems in each box in your mind, and make sure you can recall the answers instantly. Here are a couple of tips: *15^2 has been previously learned using the elegant Squaring Shortcut #1.* Also, notice how *you can memorize 13^2 and 14^2 together since their products (169 and 196) look similar to each other.*
- Next, write down your answers.
- Then, move on to the next column and repeat the two steps above. Cover up your previous answers when you move on to the next column.

G.	H.	I.	J.	K.
$11^2 =$ _____	$12^2 =$ _____	$13^2 =$ _____	$14^2 =$ _____	$15^2 =$ _____
$12^2 =$ _____	$11^2 =$ _____	$15^2 =$ _____	$13^2 =$ _____	$14^2 =$ _____
$13^2 =$ _____	$15^2 =$ _____	$12^2 =$ _____	$11^2 =$ _____	$13^2 =$ _____
$14^2 =$ _____	$13^2 =$ _____	$11^2 =$ _____	$15^2 =$ _____	$12^2 =$ _____
$15^2 =$ _____	$14^2 =$ _____	$14^2 =$ _____	$12^2 =$ _____	$11^2 =$ _____

Making Sense of Equations | © MathFluency.com | **Teachers:** Log in for demo videos.

Name_____

Lesson 28: Pythagorean Theorem

Part 1: Write the answers to the following squares, which you memorized from the previous lesson.

A. $11^2 =$	B. $12^2 =$	C. $13^2 =$	D. $14^2 =$	E. $15^2 =$

Part 2: Find the square roots.

F. $\sqrt{196} =$	G. $\sqrt{169} =$	H. $\sqrt{225} =$	I. $\sqrt{121} =$	J. $\sqrt{144} =$

Part 3: Use the Pythagorean Theorem ($a^2 + b^2 = c^2$) to find the length of the missing side. Label sides a, b, and c first (a = shortest, c = longest). Be careful since the right angle changes positions from problem to problem.

K. (triangle with sides 9, 15)

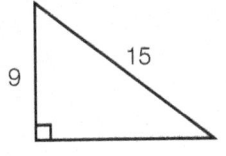

L. (triangle with sides 5, 12)

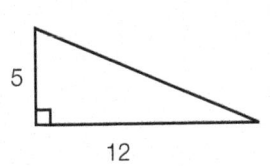

M. (triangle with sides 5, 4)

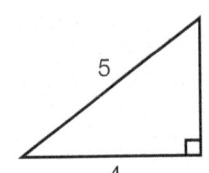

N. (triangle with sides 5, 13)

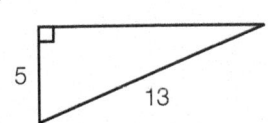

O. (triangle with sides 9, 12)

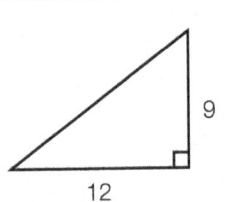

P. (triangle with sides 10, 8)

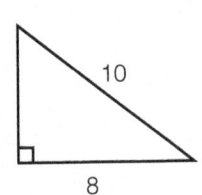

Q. (triangle with sides 5, 12)

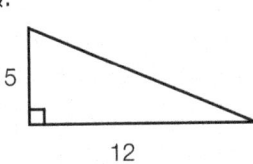

R. (triangle with sides 9, 15)

38   Making Sense of Equations | © MathFluency.com | **Teachers:** Log in for demo videos.

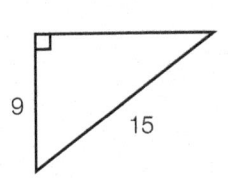

KEY LESSON

Name_____

Lesson 29: Approximating Square Roots

Part 1: Find the square roots of perfect squares.

A. $\sqrt{25} =$	B. $\sqrt{4} =$	C. $\sqrt{36} =$	D. $\sqrt{64} =$	E. $\sqrt{100} =$
F. $\sqrt{16} =$	G. $\sqrt{1} =$	H. $\sqrt{49} =$	I. $\sqrt{81} =$	J. $\sqrt{9} =$

Part 2: Follow along with your instructor to approximate square roots of non-perfect squares by approximating **down**.

K. Square root the next **smaller** perfect square.

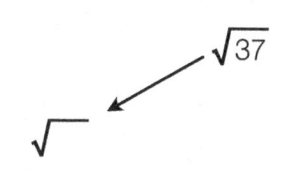

$\sqrt{37}$

$\sqrt{}$

↑ M. Check.

$\overline{\text{Step 4}}$ $\overline{\text{Step 2}}$ $\overline{\text{Step 1}}$ $\overline{\text{Step 3}}$ $\overline{\text{Step 5}}$

L. Complete the number sentence.

N. Explain in a complete sentence.

_____

_____

O. $\sqrt{17}$	P. $\sqrt{83}$
Q. $\sqrt{26}$	R. $\sqrt{5}$

Part 3: Follow along with your instructor to approximate square roots of non-perfect squares by approximating **up**.

S. Square root the next **larger** perfect square.

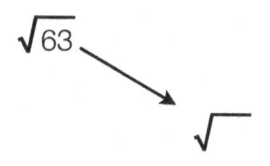

$\sqrt{63}$

$\sqrt{}$

U. Check. ↑

$\overline{\text{Step 4}}$ $\overline{\text{Step 2}}$ $\overline{\text{Step 1}}$ $\overline{\text{Step 3}}$ $\overline{\text{Step 5}}$

T. Complete the number sentence.

V. Explain in a complete sentence.

_____

_____

W. $\sqrt{47}$	X. $\sqrt{99}$
Y. $\sqrt{15}$	Z. $\sqrt{8}$

Making Sense of Equations | © MathFluency.com | **Teachers:** Log in for demo videos.

Name_____

Lesson 30: Approximating Square Roots

Part 1: Find the square roots of perfect squares.

A. $\sqrt{49} =$	B. $\sqrt{1} =$	C. $\sqrt{81} =$	D. $\sqrt{9} =$	E. $\sqrt{16} =$
F. $\sqrt{100} =$	G. $\sqrt{4} =$	H. $\sqrt{25} =$	I. $\sqrt{36} =$	J. $\sqrt{64} =$

Part 2: Follow along with your instructor to approximate square roots of non-perfect squares by approximating **up or down**. Before solving, decide whether you will approximate up or down by drawing the appropriate arrows. Indicate which integer your answer is closer to (i.e., the square root of 17 is between 4 and 5, but is closer to 4).

Example $\sqrt{17}$	K. $\sqrt{80}$	L. $\sqrt{60}$	M. $\sqrt{37}$
N. $\sqrt{3}$	O. $\sqrt{15}$	P. $\sqrt{50}$	Q. $\sqrt{103}$
R. $\sqrt{23}$	S. $\sqrt{39}$	T. $\sqrt{20}$	U. $\sqrt{18}$
V. $\sqrt{7}$	W. $\sqrt{2}$	X. $\sqrt{95}$	Y. $\sqrt{85}$

Making Sense of Equations | © MathFluency.com | Teachers: Log in for demo videos.

KEY LESSON

Lesson 31: Absolute Value

Name_____

```
◄——|——|——|——|——|——|——|——|——|——|——|——|——|——|——|——|——|——|——|——|——|——|——|——|——►
  -12 -11 -10 -9 -8 -7 -6 -5 -4 -3 -2 -1  0  1  2  3  4  5  6  7  8  9 10 11 12
```

Part 1: Follow along with your instructor to find the absolute value.

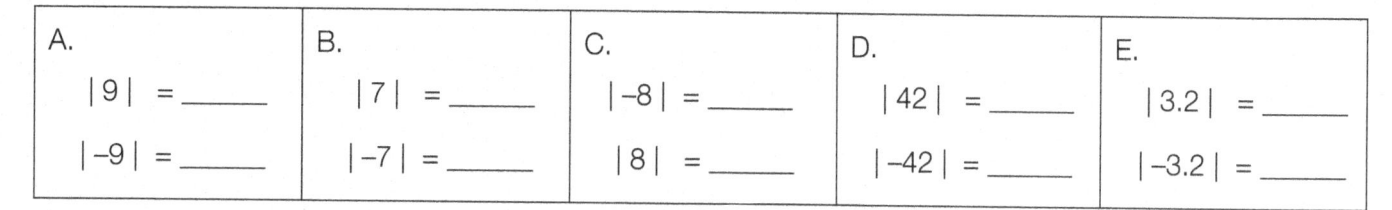

| A. $\|9\|$ = _____ $\|-9\|$ = _____ | B. $\|7\|$ = _____ $\|-7\|$ = _____ | C. $\|-8\|$ = _____ $\|8\|$ = _____ | D. $\|42\|$ = _____ $\|-42\|$ = _____ | E. $\|3.2\|$ = _____ $\|-3.2\|$ = _____ |

Part 2: Follow along with your instructor to compare parentheses versus absolute value symbols.

| F. $(-4 - 5)$ = _____ vs. $\|-4 - 5\|$ = _____ = _____ | G. $(6 - -7)$ = _____ vs. $\|6 - -7\|$ = _____ = _____ | H. $(-8 + 3)$ = _____ vs. $\|-8 + 3\|$ = _____ = _____ | I. $(-4 + 2)$ = _____ vs. $\|-4 + 2\|$ = _____ = _____ |

Part 3: Evaluate each expression.

| J. $(-5 - -2)$ | K. $(-5 + -2)$ | L. $(-5 - 2)$ | M. $(-5 + 2)$ |
| N. $(5 - -2)$ | O. $(5 + -2)$ | P. $(5 - 2)$ | Q. $(5 + 2)$ |

Part 4: Evaluate each expression.

| R. $\|-5 + -2\|$ | S. $\|-5 - -2\|$ | T. $\|-5 + 2\|$ | U. $\|-5 - 2\|$ |
| V. $\|5 + -2\|$ | W. $\|5 - -2\|$ | X. $\|5 + 2\|$ | Y. $\|5 - 2\|$ |

Making Sense of Equations | © MathFluency.com | **Teachers: Log in for demo videos.**

Name_____

Lesson 32: Absolute Value

<-- -12 -11 -10 -9 -8 -7 -6 -5 -4 -3 -2 -1 0 1 2 3 4 5 6 7 8 9 10 11 12 -->

Part 1: Follow along with your instructor to find the absolute value.

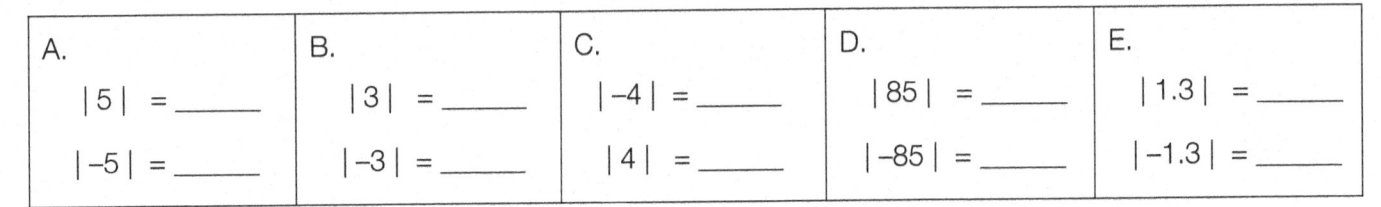

A.	B.	C.	D.	E.
$\|5\|$ = _____	$\|3\|$ = _____	$\|-4\|$ = _____	$\|85\|$ = _____	$\|1.3\|$ = _____
$\|-5\|$ = _____	$\|-3\|$ = _____	$\|4\|$ = _____	$\|-85\|$ = _____	$\|-1.3\|$ = _____

Part 2: Evaluate each expression.

Example	F.	G.
$\|-2-6\| + \|-7+3\|$	$\|2+6\| + \|7+3\|$	$\|2-6\| - \|-7+3\|$

H.	I.	J.
$\|-2-6\| - \|7+3\|$	$\|2-6\| + \|-7+3\|$	$\|2-6\| + \|7+3\|$

K.	L.	M.
$\|-2+6\| + \|-7+3\|$	$\|2+6\| - \|-7-3\|$	$\|2+6\| - \|7-3\|$

N.	O.	P.
$\|-2+6\| - \|7+3\|$	$\|2-6\| - \|-7-3\|$	$\|-2+6\| - \|-7+3\|$

Making Sense of Equations | © MathFluency.com | **Teachers: Log in for demo videos.**

Name_____

Lesson 33: Geometric Equations

Part 1: Simplify. Notice the similarities between the first row of problems and the second row of problems.

A. $n + n + n$	B. $s + s + s + s$	C. $x + x + x + x + y + y + y$	D. $z + z + z + z + z$
E. $n \cdot n \cdot n$	F. $s \cdot s \cdot s \cdot s$	G. $x \cdot x \cdot x \cdot x \cdot y \cdot y \cdot y$	H. $z \cdot z \cdot z \cdot z \cdot z$

Part 2: Factor.

I. $5d + 25e$	J. $2d + 2e$	K. $12f + 16g$	L. $2f + 2g$

Part 3: Solve. For the last row, take care of the **numbers** first, then take care of the **units**.

M. Solve for P. $s = 3$ $P = 4s$	N. Solve for P. $s = 8$ $P = 4s$	O. Solve for P. $\ell = 3, w = 5$ $P = 2(\ell + w)$	P. Solve for P. $\ell = 4, w = 6$ $P = 2(\ell + w)$
Q. Solve for A. $s = 3$ $A = s^2$	R. Solve for A. $s = 8$ $A = s^2$	S. Solve for A. $\ell = 3, w = 5$ $A = \ell \cdot w$	T. Solve for A. $\ell = 4, w = 6$ $A = \ell \cdot w$
U. Solve for P. $s = 3$ in. $P = 4s$	V. Solve for P. $\ell = 3$ in., $w = 5$ in. $P = 2(\ell + w)$	W. Solve for A. $s = 3$ in. $A = s^2$	X. Solve for A. $\ell = 3$ in., $w = 5$ in. $A = \ell \cdot w$

KEY LESSON

Name_____

Lesson 34: Difference Between Perimeter and Area of Squares and Rectangles

Part 1: Follow along with your instructor to compare the perimeter and area of a **square**.

A.

Perimeter

Meaning _____

_____

P = ____ + ____ + ____ + ____

P = ____ ____

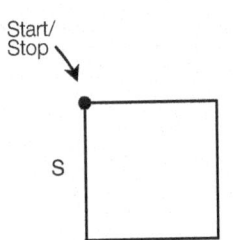

Start/Stop ↘ (square labeled s)

Area

Meaning _____

_____

A = ____

B.

Find the perimeter (include the units).

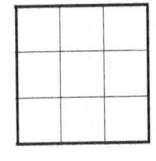

3 in. (square with grid)

Find the area (include the units).

Part 2: Follow along with your instructor to compare the perimeter and area of a **rectangle**.

C.

Perimeter

P = ____ + ____ + ____ + ____

P = ____ + ____ + ____ + ____

P = ____ ____ + ____ ____

P = _____

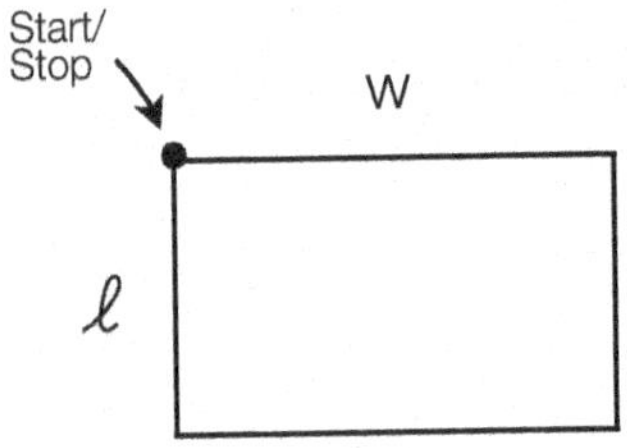

Start/Stop ↘ (rectangle with w on top, ℓ on side)

Area

A = ____ · ____

D.

Find the perimeter (include the units).

5 in.

3 in. (rectangle with grid)

Find the area (include the units).

44 Making Sense of Equations | © MathFluency.com | Teachers: Log in for demo videos.

Name_____

Lesson 35: Perimeter and Area of Squares and Rectangles

Part 1: Find the perimeter and area of each **square**.

A.
Find the perimeter (include the units).   Find the area (include the units).

5 mi

B.
Find the perimeter (include the units).   Find the area (include the units).

15 cm

Part 2: Find the perimeter and area of each **rectangle**.

C.
Find the perimeter (include the units).   5 in   Find the area (include the units).

10 in

D.
Find the perimeter (include the units).   Find the area (include the units).

2 yd
8 yd

Making Sense of Equations | © MathFluency.com | **Teachers: Log in for demo videos.**

KEY LESSON

Lesson 36: Geometric Word Problems

Directions: Follow along with your instructor to answer the questions about the rectangular pool below. **All four corners of the pool are right angles and measure 90°.** Include the correct units (ft or ft²) in all your answers.

A. Find the perimeter of the pool.	B. Find the area of the pool.
C. A swimmer swims the length of the pool (40 ft) eight times. What was the total distance that she swam?	D. A swimmer swims diagonally across the pool from one corner to the opposite corner, as shown in the diagram. How far did she swim?

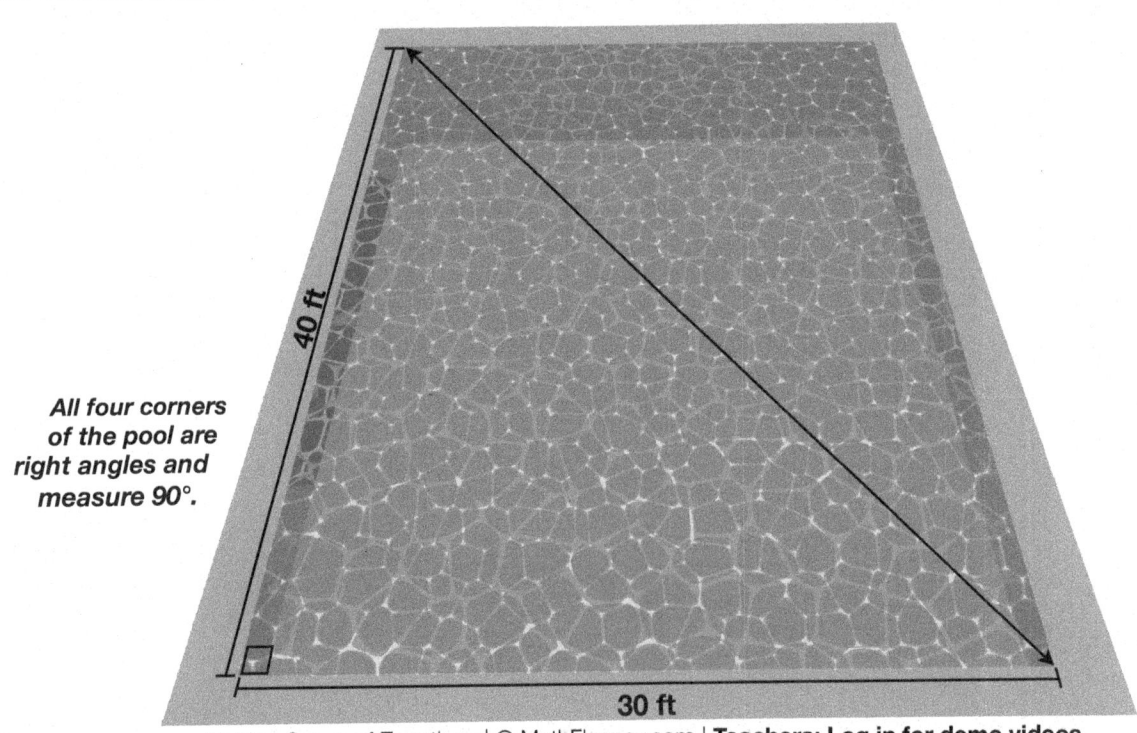

All four corners of the pool are right angles and measure 90°.

40 ft

30 ft

Making Sense of Equations | © MathFluency.com | **Teachers: Log in for demo videos.**

KEY LESSON

Name_____

Lesson 37: Difference Between Perimeter and Area of Rectangles and Triangles

Part 1: Simplify, then multiply.

| A. $\frac{1}{5} \times 25 = $ ___ | B. $\frac{1}{2} \times 8 = $ ___ | C. $\frac{1}{2} \times 6 = $ ___ |

Part 2: Follow along with your instructor to derive the formula for the perimeter and the area of a triangle.

D.
Rectangle   Area

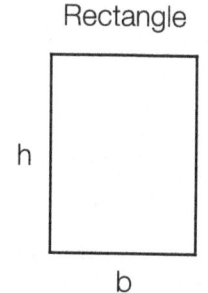

h
b

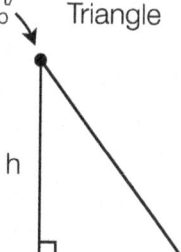

E.
Perimeter   Triangle (Start/Stop)   Area

P = ___ + ___ + ___

h
b

A = ___ ___ · ___

Part 3: Follow along with your instructor to calculate the perimeter and area of a triangle.

F.
Rectangle   Find the area.

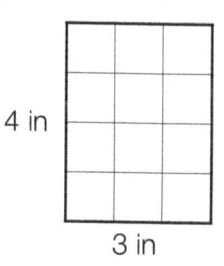

4 in
3 in

G. Find the perimeter.   Triangle   Find the area.

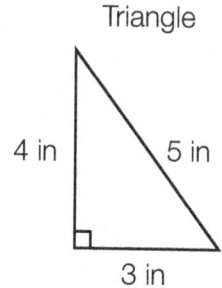

4 in   5 in
3 in

Making Sense of Equations | © MathFluency.com | **Teachers: Log in for demo videos.** 47

KEY LESSON

Name_____

Lesson 38: Area of Triangles (page 1 of 3)

Part 1: Find the base and the height of each triangle (use a solid line for the base and a dotted line for the height, and be sure to corner the right angle). The lengths or approximate lengths of some of the sides are provided as reference.

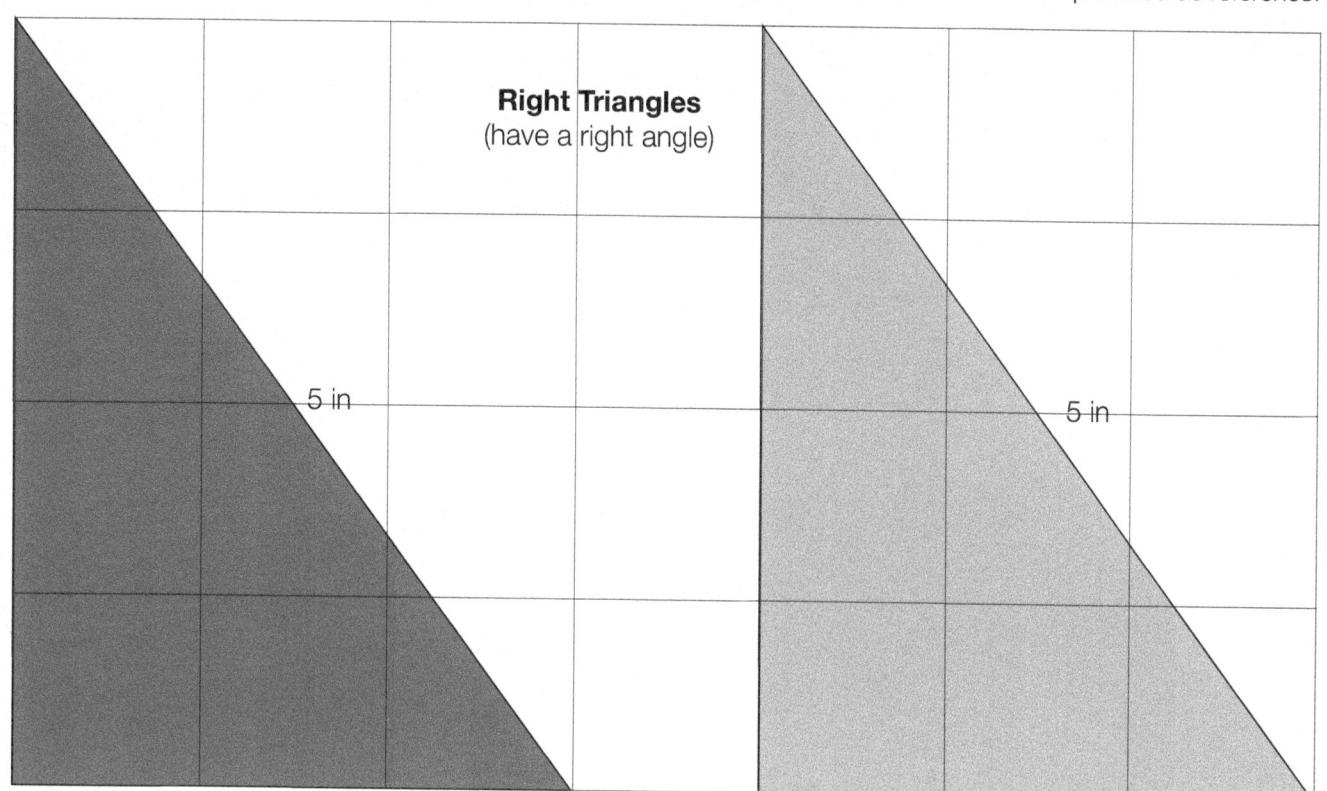

Right Triangles
(have a right angle)

5 in

5 in

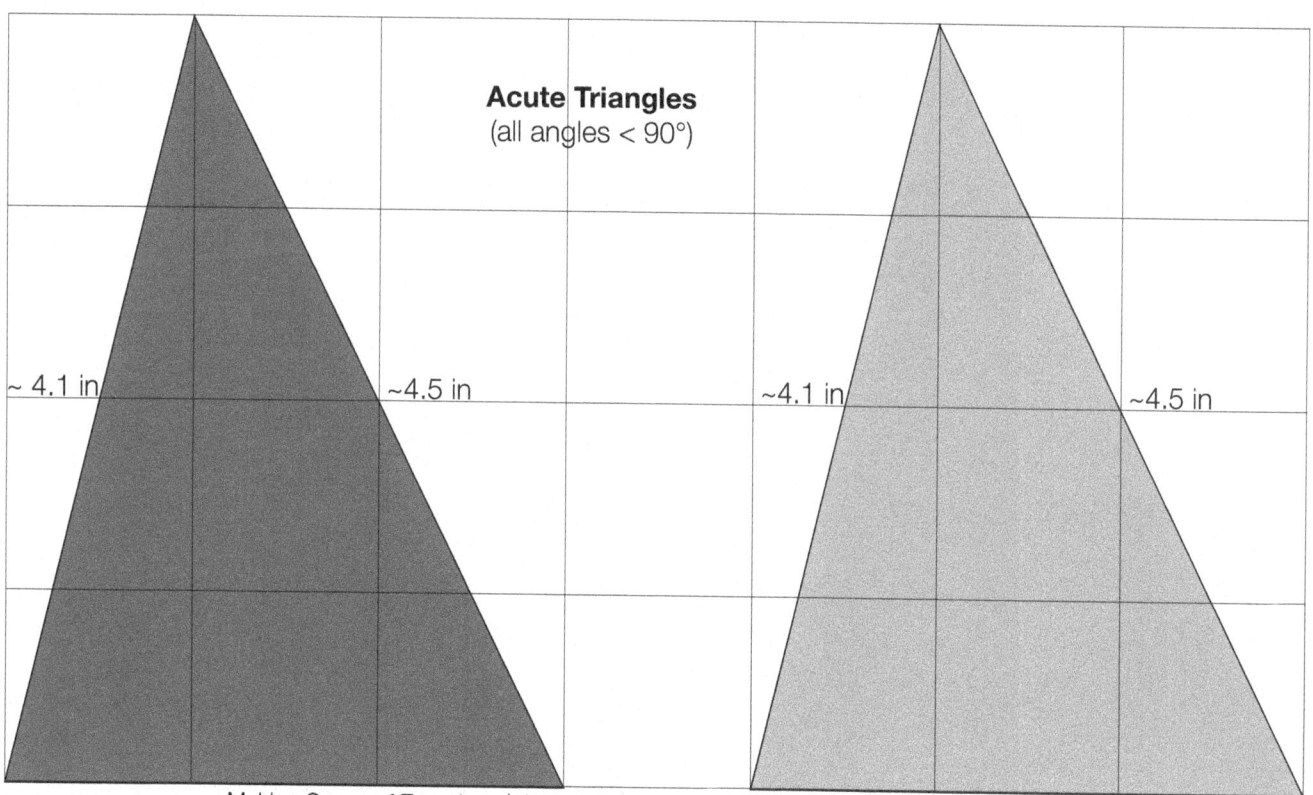

Acute Triangles
(all angles < 90°)

~ 4.1 in   ~4.5 in   ~4.1 in   ~4.5 in

Making Sense of Equations | © MathFluency.com | **Teachers: Log in for demo videos.**

Lesson 38: Area of Triangles (page 2 of 3)

Part 1 (continued): Find the base and the height of each triangle (use a solid line for the base and a dotted line for the height, and be sure to corner the right angle). The lengths or approximate lengths of some of the sides are provided as reference.

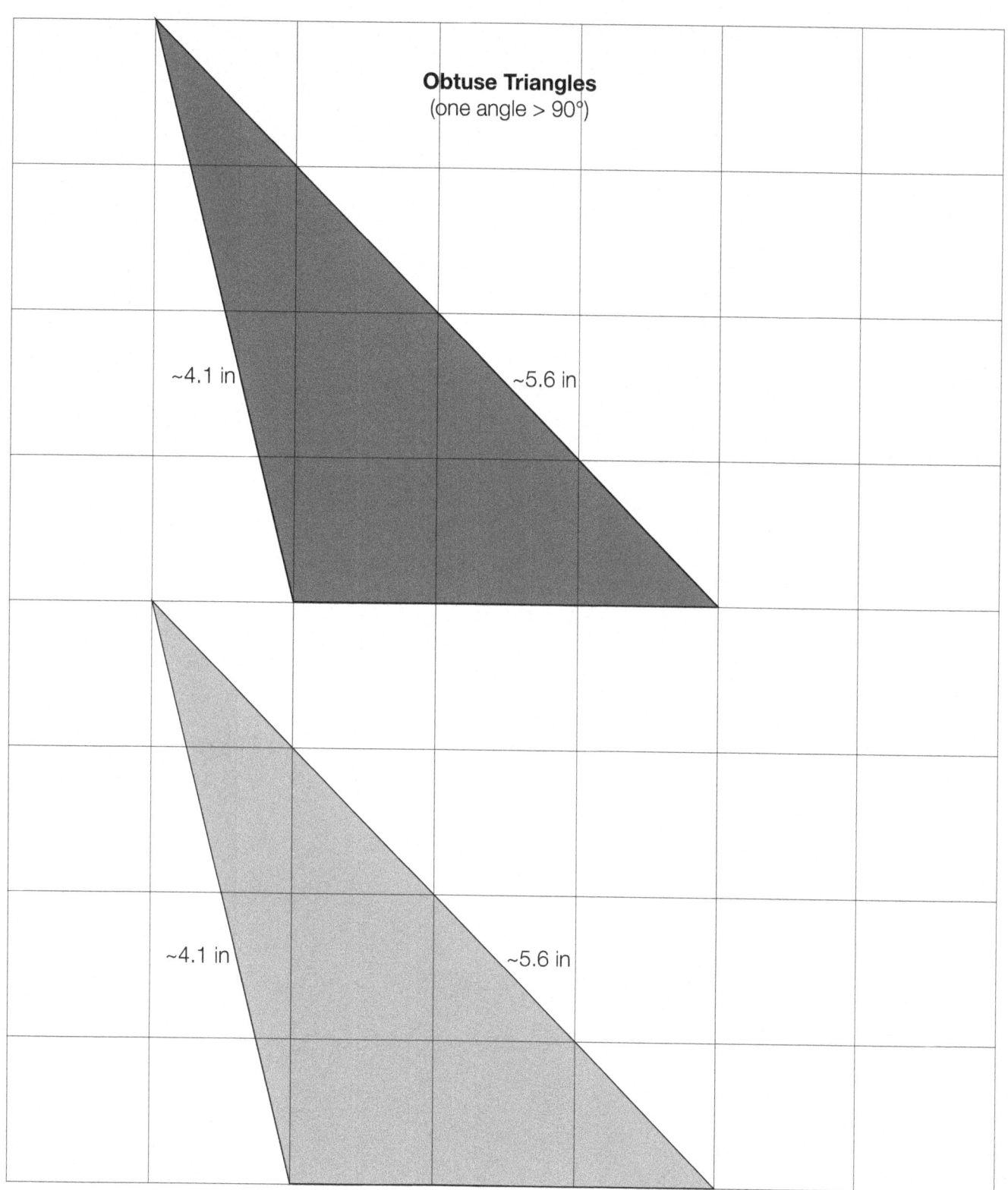

Obtuse Triangles
(one angle > 90°)

~4.1 in ~5.6 in

~4.1 in ~5.6 in

Lesson 38: Area of Triangles (page 3 of 3)

Part 2: Use the grids below to find the area of each triangle on the previous pages indicated below.

Right Triangle (dark grey, has a right angle)
(Use the light grey triangle to help you.)

Acute Triangle (dark grey, all angles < 90°)
(Use the light grey triangle to help you.)

Obtuse Triangle (dark grey, one angle > 90°)
(Use the light grey triangle to help you.)

Workspace

Area of Right Triangle

Area of Acute Triangle

Area of Obtuse Triangle

Lesson 39: Perimeter and Area of Triangles

Instructions: Find the perimeter ($P = s_1 + s_2 + s_3$) and the area ($A = 1/2\ bh$) of each triangle. Include the units.

Triangle (4.1 m, 4.5 m, 4 m height, 3 m base)	A. Perimeter	B. Area
Triangle (4.4 in, 5.6 in, 4 in height, 6 in base)	C. Perimeter	D. Area
Triangle (4 m, 5.7 m, 4.1 m, 3 m base)	E. Perimeter	F. Area
Triangle (6 ft, 10 ft, 8 ft)	G. Perimeter	H. Area
Triangle (8.4 mi, 8.4 mi, 6 mi height, 12 mi base)	I. Perimeter	J. Area

KEY LESSON

Name_____

Lesson 40: Pythagorean Theorem; Perimeter and Area of Triangles

Part 1: In Box A, use the Pythagorean Theorem ($a^2 + b^2 = c^2$) to find the length of the missing side. Then, use your solution from Box A to find the perimeter ($P = s_1 + s_2 + s_3$) and area ($A = 1/2\ bh$).

A. Use the Pythagorean Theorem to find the length of the missing side. 3 cm 5 cm	B. Find the perimeter.
	C. Find the area.

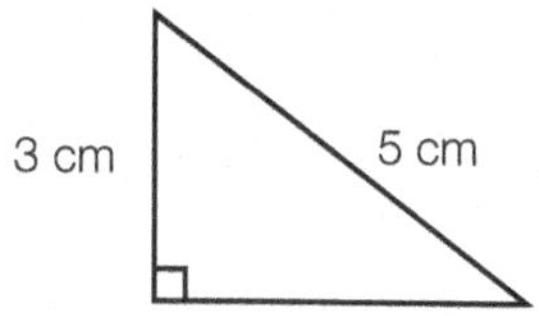

Part 2: Find the length of the missing side. Then, find the perimeter and area.

D. Use the Pythagorean Theorem to find the length of the missing side. 6 m 10 m	E. Find the perimeter.
	F. Find the area.

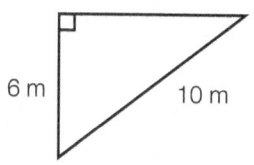

Part 3: Find the length of the missing side. Then, find the perimeter and area.

G. Use the Pythagorean Theorem to find the length of the missing side. 13 m 12 m	H. Find the perimeter.
	I. Find the area.

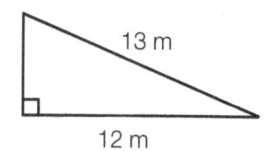

Making Sense of Equations | © MathFluency.com | **Teachers: Log in for demo videos.**

Lesson 41: Area of Parallelograms (page 1 of 2)

Part 1: Find the base and the height of the parallelogram (use a solid line for the base and a dotted line for the height, and be sure to corner the right angle). The approximate lengths of some of the sides are provided as reference.

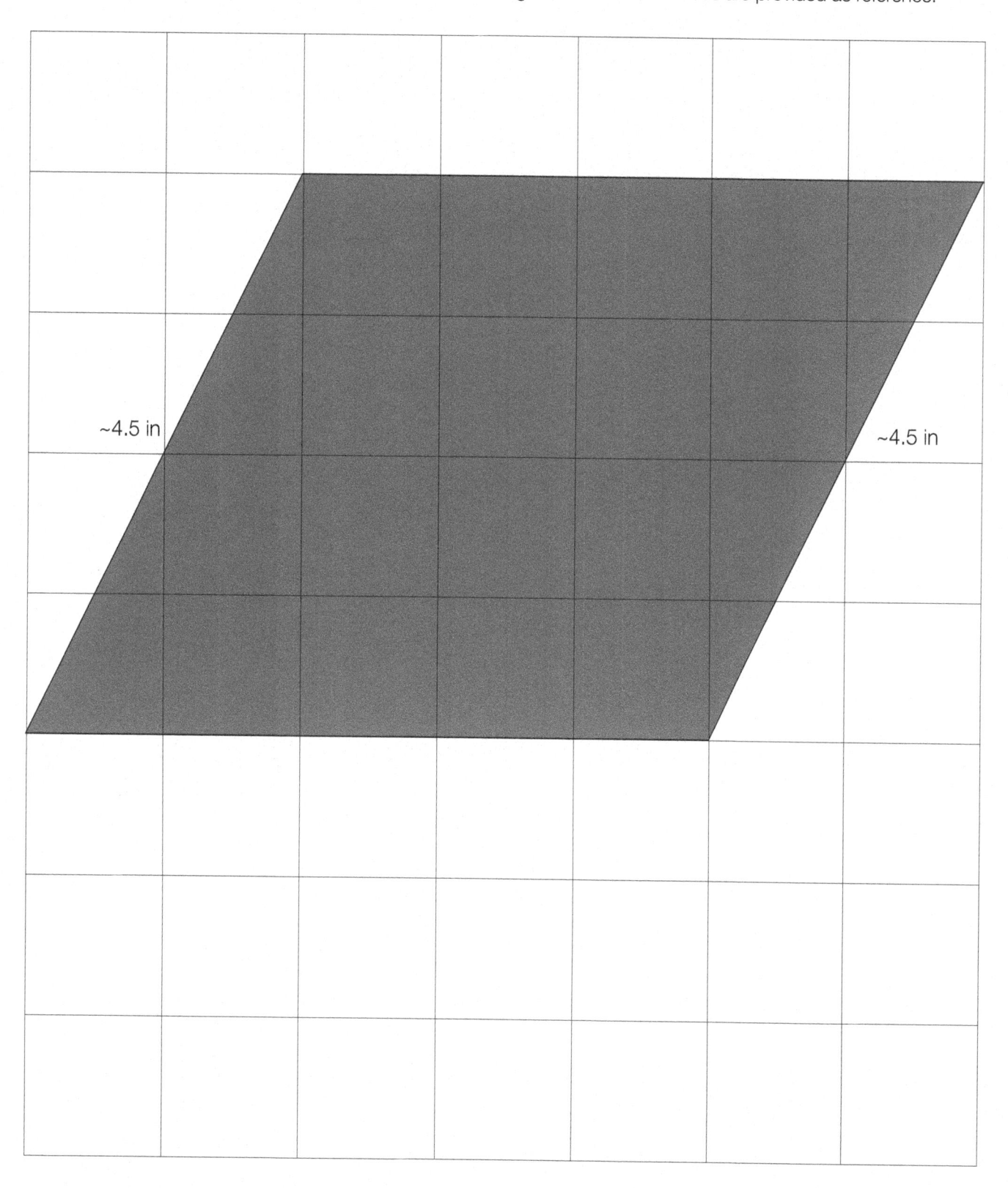

~4.5 in

~4.5 in

Making Sense of Equations | © MathFluency.com | **Teachers: Log in for demo videos.**

Name_____

Lesson 41: Area of Parallelograms (Page 2 of 2)

Part 2: Find the base and height of the parallelogram on the preceding page (use a dotted line for the height, and be sure to corner the right angle). Then, use the grid below to find the area of the parallelogram.

Workspace

Area of Parallelogram

Lesson 42: Perimeter and Area of Parallelograms

Instructions: Use the formulas $P = 2(s_1 + s_2)$ and $A = bh$ to find the perimeter and area. Include the units.

3.6 m, 3 m, 5 m	A. Perimeter	B. Area
3.2 ft, 3 ft, 4 ft	C. Perimeter	D. Area
8.2 in, 8 in, 8 in	E. Perimeter	F. Area
6.4 cm, 6 cm, 4 cm	G. Perimeter	H. Area
6.7 m, 6 m, 3 m	I. Perimeter	J. Area

Lesson 43: Area of Trapezoids (page 1 of 2)

Part 1: Find the bases and the heights of each trapezoid (use a solid line for the bases and a dotted line for the heights, and be sure to corner the right angle). The approximate lengths of some of the sides are provided as reference.

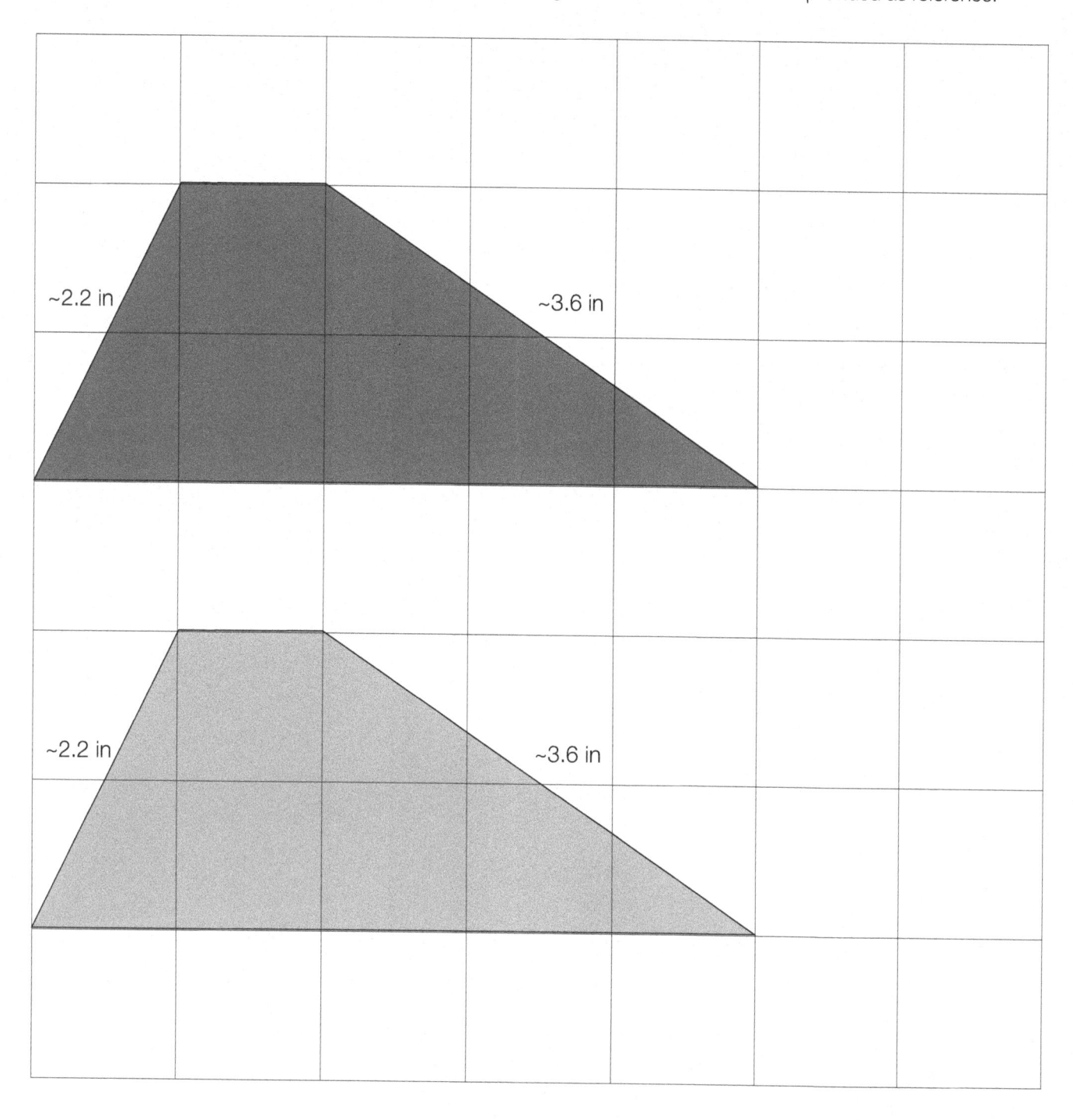

~2.2 in ~3.6 in

~2.2 in ~3.6 in

Name_____

Lesson 43: Area of Trapezoids (page 2 of 2)

Part 2: Find the bases and heights of the trapezoids on the preceding page (use a dotted line for the height, and be sure to corner the right angle). Then, use the grid below to find the area of trapezoids.

Workspace

Area of Trapezoid

Name_____

Lesson 44: Trapezoid Equations

Part 1: Add. Use the empty white space to rewrite each problem vertically, and be sure to line up your decimal points.

A. 2.1 + 1 + 2.8 + 4 = _____

B. 3.4 + 1 + 5.6 + 7 = _____

C. 1.8 + 4.3 + 10 + 7.3 = _____

D. 3.9 + 1 + 6 + 4 = _____

Part 2: Simplify. Combine like terms in the parentheses (think back to the "Apples + Apples" lesson). Then, **simplify fractions before multiplying.** Remember to include the units in your calculations and in your answers.

E. $\frac{1}{2} \cdot 3\text{ m }(1\text{ m} + 5\text{ m})$	F. $\frac{1}{2} \cdot 4\text{ cm }(3\text{ cm} + 4\text{ cm})$	G. $\frac{1}{2} \cdot 7\text{ km }(2\text{ km} + 4\text{ km})$
H. $\frac{1}{2} \cdot 6\text{ in }(2\text{ in} + 4\text{ in})$	I. $\frac{1}{2} \cdot 5\text{ yd }(3\text{ yd} + 7\text{ yd})$	J. $\frac{1}{2} \cdot 3\text{ mi }(8\text{ mi} + 6\text{ mi})$
K. $\frac{1}{2} \cdot 10\text{ ft }(2\text{ ft} + 3\text{ ft})$	L. $\frac{1}{2} \cdot 9\text{ m }(4\text{ m} + 6\text{ m})$	M. $\frac{1}{2} \cdot 8\text{ in }(3\text{ in} + 2\text{ in})$

Name_____

Lesson 45: Perimeter and Area of Trapezoids

Instructions: Use the formulas $P = s_1 + s_2 + s_3 + s_4$ and $A = 1/2\ h(b_1 + b_2)$ to find the perimeter and area.

Trapezoid: top 1 km, left side 2.2 km, height 2 km, right side 2.8 km, bottom 4 km	A. Perimeter	B. Area
Trapezoid: top 1 m, left side 4.1 m, height 4 m, right side 5 m, bottom 5 m	C. Perimeter	D. Area
Trapezoid: top 3 cm, left side 2.2 cm, height 2 cm, right side 2.2 cm, bottom 5 cm	E. Perimeter	F. Area
Trapezoid: top 2 ft, left side 4.5 ft, height 4 ft, right side 4.1 ft, bottom 5 ft	G. Perimeter	H. Area
Trapezoid: top 4 yd, left side 10 yd, height 8 yd, right side 8 yd, bottom 10 yd	I. Perimeter	J. Area

Making Sense of Equations | © MathFluency.com | **Teachers:** Log in for demo videos.

KEY LESSON
Lesson 46: Why Pi?

Part 1: Follow along with your instructor to learn the formula for the **circumference** of a circle.

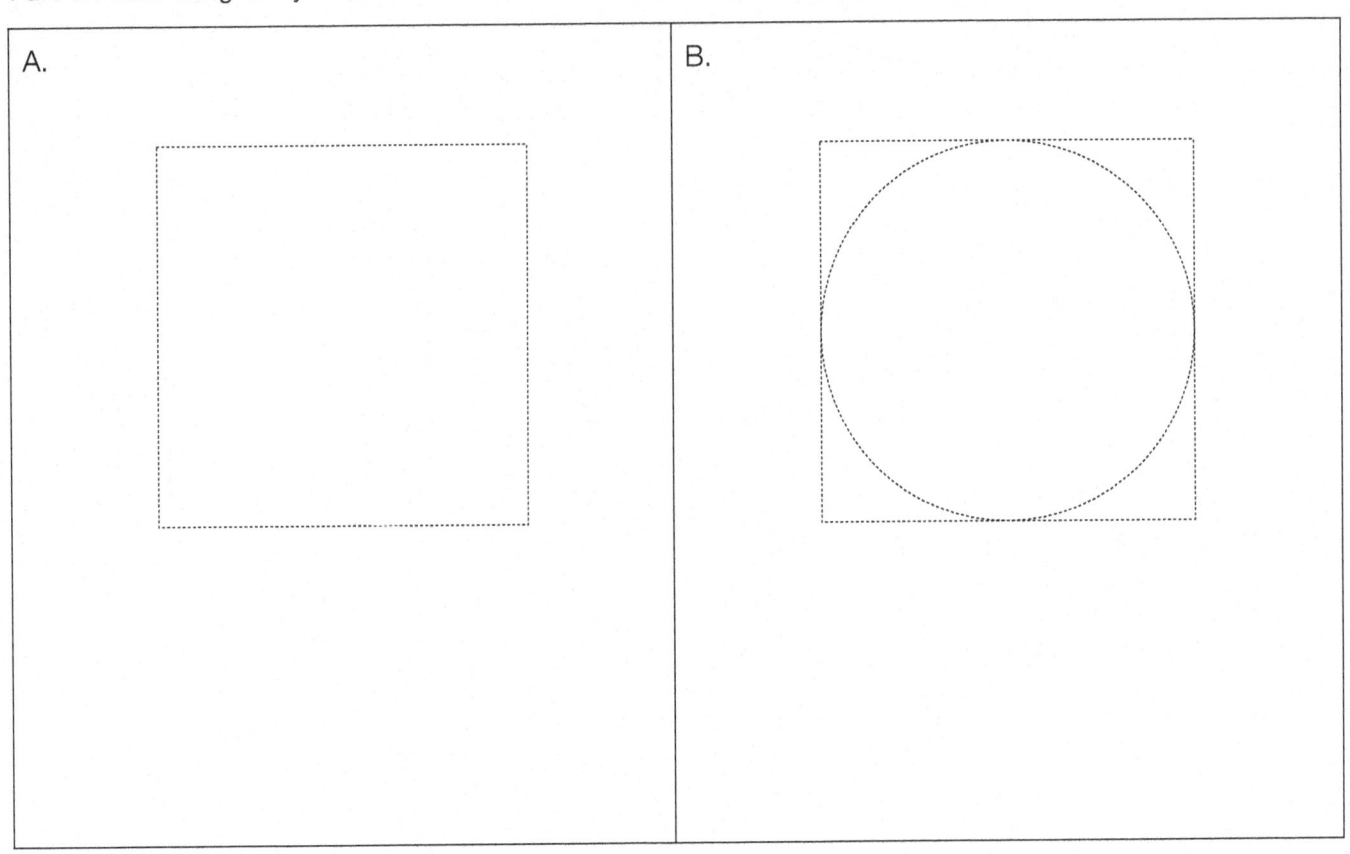

A.

B.

Part 2: Follow along with your instructor to learn the formula for the **area** of a circle.

C.

D.

66   Making Sense of Equations | © MathFluency.com | **Teachers: Log in for demo videos.**

Name_____

Lesson 47: Circumference and Area

Directions: Follow along with your instructor to find the circumference and area of each circle. Include the units.

A circle has a radius of 3 inches. r = d =	A. Circumference	B. Area
A circle has a diameter of 8 meters. r = d =	C. Circumference	D. Area
A circle has a diameter of 40 meters. r = d =	E. Circumference	F. Area
A circle has a radius of 5 inches. r = d =	G. Circumference	H. Area

Name_____

Lesson 48: Circumference and Area (Leave Answers in Terms of π)

Directions: Find the circumference and area. Leave your answers in terms of π. Include the units.

A circle has a radius of 45 miles. r = d =	A. Circumference	B. Area
A circle has a diameter of 32 yards. r = d =	C. Circumference	D. Area
A circle has a radius of 5 inches. r = d =	E. Circumference	F. Area
A circle has a radius of 65 yards. r = d =	G. Circumference	H. Area

KEY LESSON

Name_____

Lesson 49: Volume of Cubes and Rectangular Prisms

Directions: Follow along with your instructor to complete this lesson. Find the area or volume. Include the units.

Two Dimensions ( )	Three Dimensions ( )
A. List the two dimensions: _____, _____ Name of Base shape: _____ Find the area: _____ 2 in / 2 in (square)	B. List the three dimensions: _____, _____, _____ Name of solid figure: _____ Find the volume: _____ 2 in / 2 in / 2 in (cube)
C. List the two dimensions: _____, _____ Name of Base shape: _____ Find the area: _____ 2 in / 3 in (rectangle)	D. List the three dimensions: _____, _____, _____ Name of solid figure: _____ Find the volume: _____ 2 in / 3 in / 2 in (rectangular prism)

Making Sense of Equations | © MathFluency.com | **Teachers:** Log in for demo videos.

Name_____

Lesson 50: Volume of Cubes and Rectangular Prisms

Directions: Name each solid figure. Then, find the volume. Remember to include the units in both your calculations and in your answer. Use **length, width,** and **height** as your three dimensions.

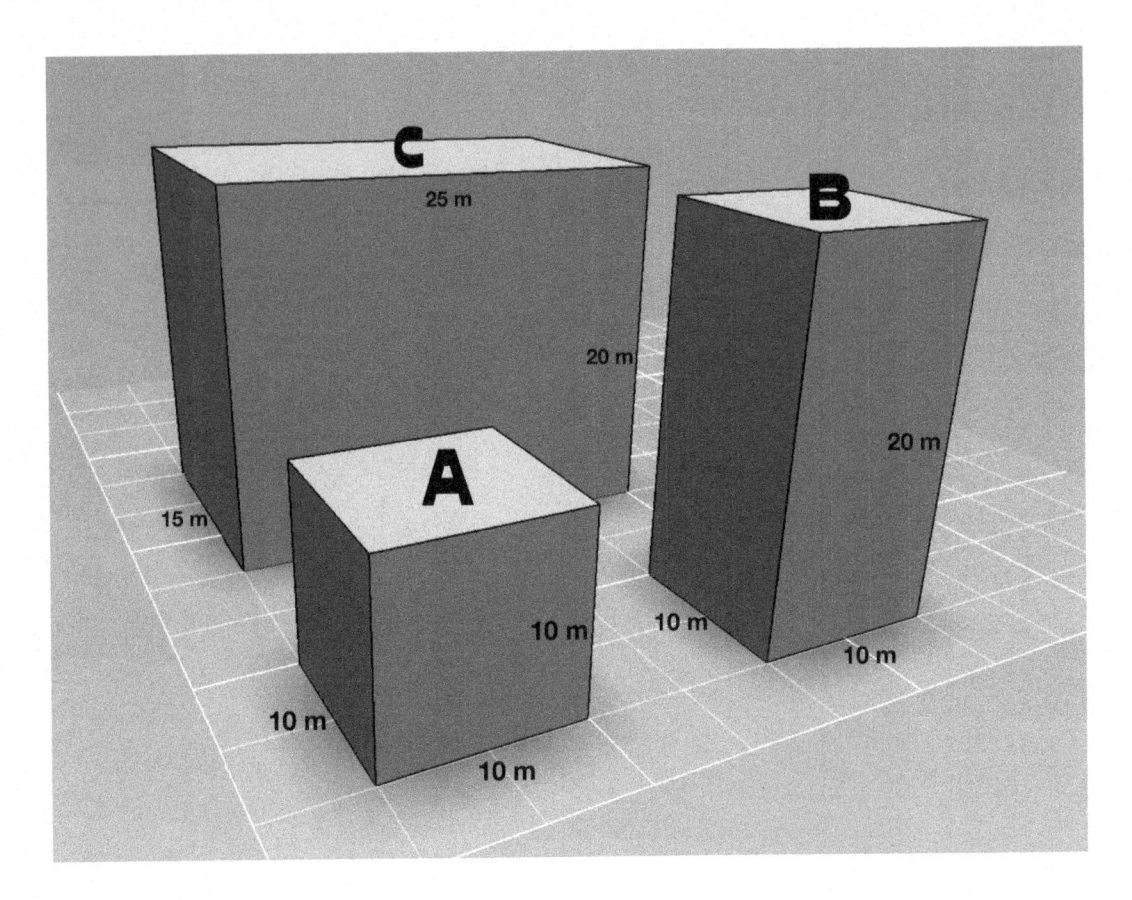

A.	B.	C.
Name of Solid A: _____	Name of Solid B: _____	Name of Solid C: _____
Volume:	Volume:	Volume:

Name_____

Lesson 51: Volume of Triangular Prisms

Directions: Follow along with your instructor to complete this lesson. Find the area or volume.

Two Dimensions ( )	Three Dimensions ( )
A. List the two dimensions: _____, _____ Name of Base shape: _____ Find the area: 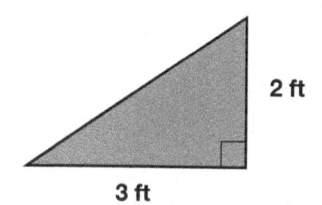 _____ *[Right triangle: 3 ft base, 2 ft height]*	**B.** List the three dimensions: _____, _____, _____ Name of solid figure: _____ Find the volume: 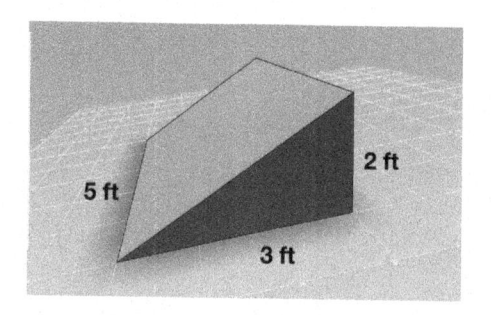 _____ *[Triangular prism: 5 ft, 2 ft, 3 ft]*
C. List the two dimensions: _____, _____ Name of Base shape: _____ Find the area: 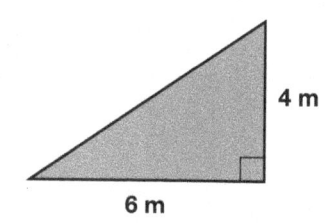 _____ *[Right triangle: 6 m base, 4 m height]*	**D.** List the three dimensions: _____, _____, _____ Name of solid figure: _____ Find the volume: 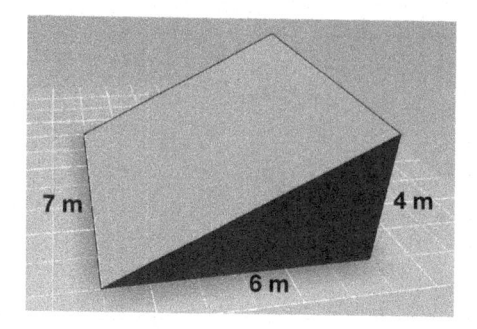 _____ *[Triangular prism: 7 m, 4 m, 6 m]*

Making Sense of Equations | © MathFluency.com | Teachers: Log in for demo videos.

KEY LESSON

Name_____

Lesson 52: Variables on Both Sides of the Equation

Part 1: Follow along with your instructor to solve the two equations using Method 1 and Method 2.

A. Method 1: Subtract 5x from both sides first. $$5x - 8 = 2x + 4$$	B. Method 2: Subtract 2x from both sides first. $$5x - 8 = 2x + 4$$

Both Method 1 and Method 2 gave you _____ _____ _____.

Which method helped you avoid using negative coefficients? _____ _____

Part 2: Solve. Hint: "Stay positive." You need to decide whether to move all the variables to either the left side or the right side of the equation. For these problems, choose the side that helps you keep the coefficients positive.

C. $$3x = x + 6$$	D. $$2x + 15 = 5x$$	E. $$2x + 4 = -3x + 34$$
F. $$x + 6 = 3x - 2$$	G. $$-2x - 11 = -5x + 10$$	H. $$-3x = 2x + 20$$

72   Making Sense of Equations | © MathFluency.com | **Teachers:** Log in for demo videos.

KEY LESSON

Name_____

Lesson 53: Variables on Both Sides of the Equation

Part 1: Follow along with your instructor to solve the two equations using Method 1 and Method 2.

A. Method 1 – Use the Distributive Property first. $8x = 4(x + 5)$	B. Method 2 – Simplify first (divide both sides by 4). $8x = 4(x + 5)$

Both Method 1 and Method 2 gave you _____ _____ _____.

Which method helped you avoid working with large numbers? _____ _____

Part 2: Solve. Hint: It's often easier to simplify first.

C. $12x = 4(x + 6)$	D. $2(x + 16) = 6x$
E. Simplify first. Then, keep the variable on the left side of the equation since the only constant of 9 will already be on the right. $-6y = 2(y + 9)$	F. Use the Distributive Property first since $-3x + 34$ is not divisible by 2. $2(x + 2) = -3x + 34$

KEY LESSON

Name_____

Lesson 54: Multi-Step Equations

Directions: Follow along with your instructor to solve each equation..

A. $72 = 6x + 3x$	B. $3x + 5x - 2 = 54$	C. $11x - 2x + 4 = 10$
D. Use the Distributive Property first. $11 = -4(-6x - 3)$	E. Solve by inspection. $\dfrac{3}{-7(40-5)} = \dfrac{x}{-7(40-5)}$	F. Solve by inspection. $-6 = -(x + 4)$
G. $\dfrac{8x - 1}{3} = 5$	H. $\dfrac{3x - 1}{2} = x + 3$	I. $-6 = \dfrac{4x + 6}{5}$
J. $\dfrac{1}{8}x + \dfrac{1}{4} = 2$	K. $\dfrac{1}{9}x + \dfrac{1}{3} = \dfrac{2}{3}$	L. $\dfrac{1}{2}x = 2x - 12$

Making Sense of Equations | © MathFluency.com | **Teachers:** Log in for demo videos.

Answer Keys and Correcting Student Work

The answer keys in this section are fully annotated. They not only show the correct answer, but also how to get there. This makes is easier to troubleshoot student errors so that they can correct them.

Provide immediate feedback so that students know how they are doing. Take a look at the sample work below.

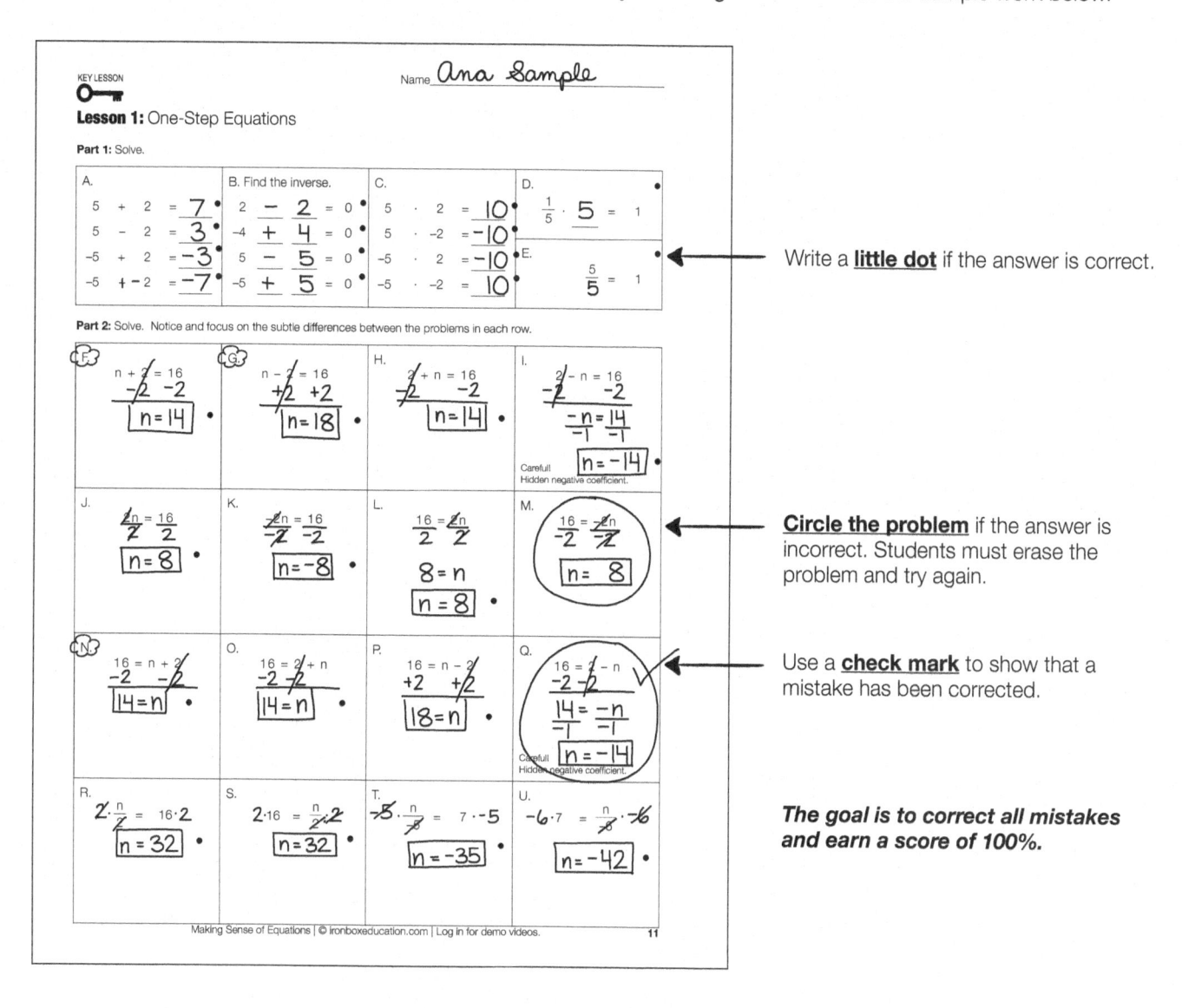

→ Write a **little dot** if the answer is correct.

→ **Circle the problem** if the answer is incorrect. Students must erase the problem and try again.

→ Use a **check mark** to show that a mistake has been corrected.

The goal is to correct all mistakes and earn a score of 100%.

Lesson 1: One-Step Equations

Part 1: Solve.

A.
$5 + 2 = 7$
$5 - 2 = 3$
$-5 + 2 = -3$
$-5 - 2 = -7$

B. Find the inverse.
$2 - 2 = 0$
$-4 + 4 = 0$
$5 - 5 = 0$
$-5 + 5 = 0$

C.
$5 \cdot 2 = 10$
$5 \cdot -2 = -10$
$-5 \cdot 2 = -10$
$-5 \cdot -2 = 10$

D. $\frac{1}{5} \cdot 5 = 1$

E. $\frac{5}{5} = 1$

Part 2: Solve. Notice and focus on the subtle differences between the problems in each row.

F. $n + 2 = 16$; $-2\ -2$; $n = 14$

G. $n - 2 = 16$; $+2\ +2$; $n = 18$

H. $2 + n = 16$; $-2\ -2$; $n = 14$

I. $2 - n = 16$; $-2\ -2$; $-n = 14$; $\frac{-n}{-1} = \frac{14}{-1}$; $n = -14$ (Careful! Hidden negative coefficient.)

J. $\frac{2n}{2} = \frac{16}{2}$; $n = 8$

K. $\frac{2n}{-2} = \frac{16}{-2}$; $n = -8$

L. $\frac{16}{2} = \frac{2n}{2}$; $8 = n$; $n = 8$

M. $\frac{16}{-2} = \frac{2n}{-2}$; $n = -8$

N. $16 = n + 2$; $-2\ -2$; $14 = n$

O. $16 = 2 + n$; $-2\ -2$; $14 = n$

P. $16 = n - 2$; $+2\ +2$; $18 = n$

Q. $16 = 2 - n$; $-2\ -2$; $\frac{14}{-1} = \frac{-n}{-1}$; $n = -14$ (Careful! Hidden negative coefficient.)

R. $2 \cdot \frac{n}{2} = 16 \cdot 2$; $n = 32$

S. $2 \cdot 16 = \frac{n}{2} \cdot 2$; $n = 32$

T. $-5 \cdot \frac{n}{-5} = 7 \cdot -5$; $n = -35$

U. $-6 \cdot 7 = \frac{n}{-6} \cdot -6$; $n = -42$

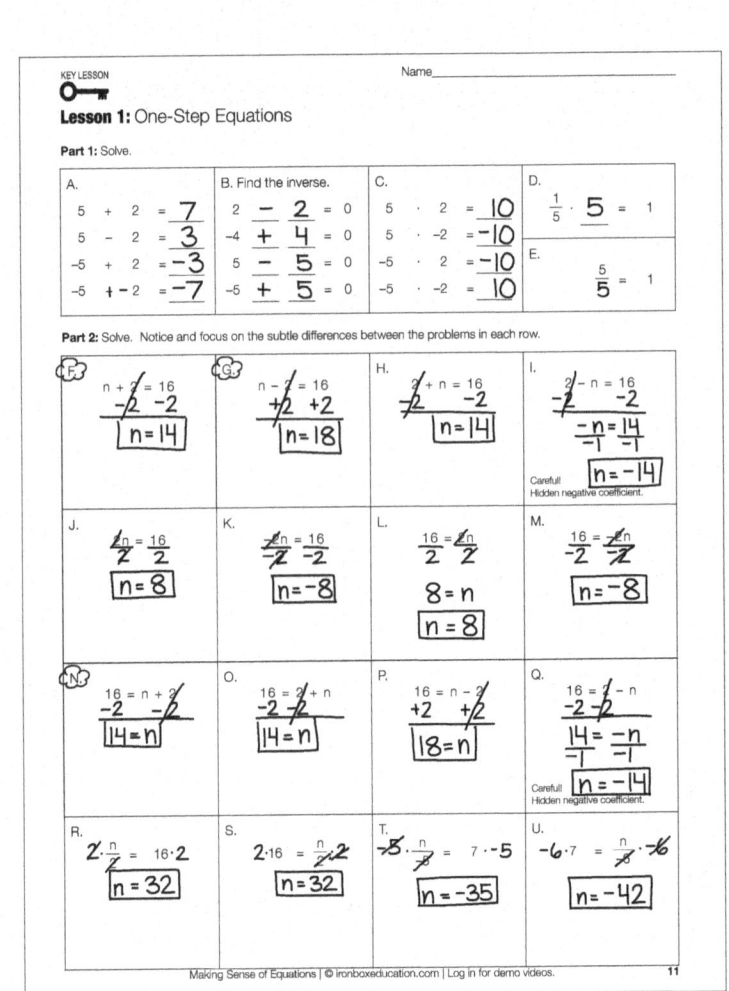

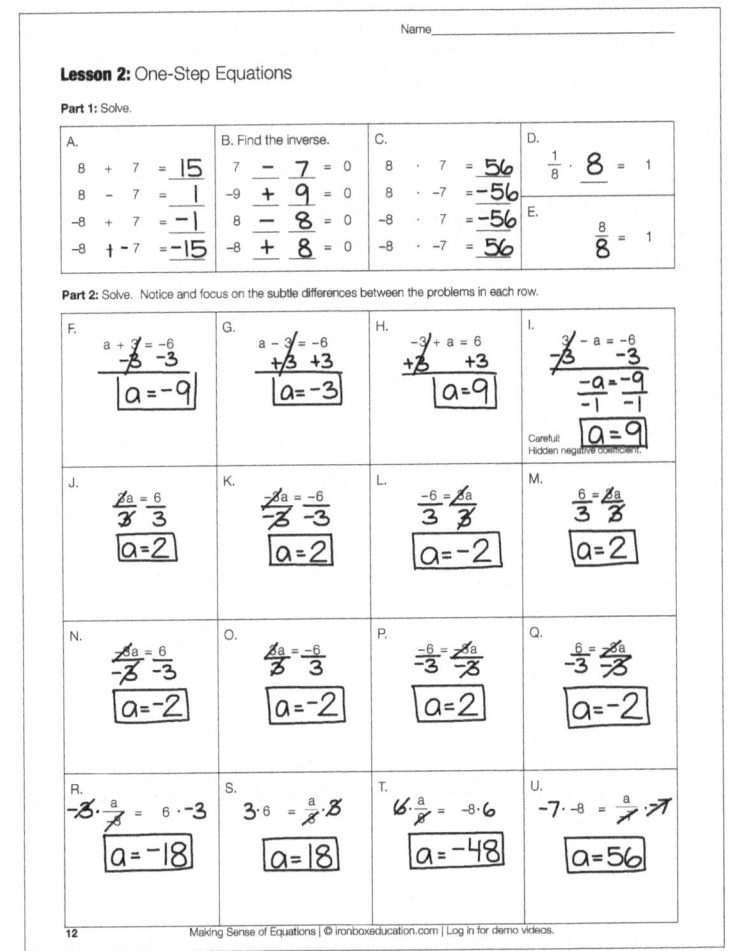

Key Points from Demo Video – Lesson 1
One-Step Equations

One-step equations may sound simple enough, but they can actually be tricky for students because even a single step can involve one of many possibilities:

- add, subtract, multiply, or divide
- positive or negative values
- variable on the left or right of the equal sign

Part 1 reviews prerequisite skills, including adding, subtracting, multiplying, and dividing integers.

In Part 2, students solve each equation, as shown in the demo video. **Notice and focus on the subtle differences between the problems.** For example, notice how Box F and Box G differ:

- $n + 2 = 16$
- $n - 2 = 16$

Also, notice how Box F and Box N differ:

- $n + 2 = 16$
- $16 = n + 2$

This lesson focuses on these little details that can have a big impact on the solution.

Lesson 2: One-Step Equations

Part 1: Solve.

A.
$8 + 7 = 15$
$8 - 7 = 1$
$-8 + 7 = -1$
$-8 - 7 = -15$

B. Find the inverse.
$7 - 7 = 0$
$-9 + 9 = 0$
$8 - 8 = 0$
$-8 + 8 = 0$

C.
$8 \cdot 7 = 56$
$8 \cdot -7 = -56$
$-8 \cdot 7 = -56$
$-8 \cdot -7 = 56$

D. $\frac{1}{8} \cdot 8 = 1$

E. $\frac{8}{8} = 1$

Part 2: Solve. Notice and focus on the subtle differences between the problems in each row.

F. $a + 3 = -6$; $-3\ -3$; $a = -9$

G. $a - 3 = -6$; $+3\ +3$; $a = -3$

H. $-3 + a = -6$; $+3\ +3$; $a = 9$

I. $3 - a = -6$; $-3\ -3$; $\frac{-a}{-1} = \frac{-9}{-1}$; $a = 9$ (Careful! Hidden negative coefficient.)

J. $\frac{3a}{3} = \frac{6}{3}$; $a = 2$

K. $\frac{3a}{-3} = \frac{-6}{-3}$; $a = 2$

L. $\frac{-6}{3} = \frac{3a}{3}$; $a = -2$

M. $\frac{6}{3} = \frac{3a}{3}$; $a = 2$

N. $\frac{3a}{-3} = \frac{6}{-3}$; $a = -2$

O. $\frac{3a}{3} = \frac{-6}{3}$; $a = -2$

P. $\frac{-6}{-3} = \frac{3a}{-3}$; $a = 2$

Q. $\frac{6}{-3} = \frac{3a}{-3}$; $a = -2$

R. $-3 \cdot \frac{a}{-3} = 6 \cdot -3$; $a = -18$

S. $3 \cdot 6 = \frac{a}{3} \cdot 3$; $a = 18$

T. $6 \cdot \frac{a}{6} = -8 \cdot 6$; $a = -48$

U. $-7 \cdot -8 = \frac{a}{-7} \cdot -7$; $a = 56$

Key Points from Demo Video – Lesson 2
One-Step Equations

As was shown in Lesson 1, even one-step equations can be tricky because a single step can involve one of many possibilities. In Lesson 2, students continue working with the many variations they will encounter working with one-step equations.

Part 1 reviews prerequisite skills, including adding, subtracting, multiplying, and dividing integers.

In Part 2, students solve each equation, as shown in the demo video. Notice and focus on the subtle differences between the problems. For example, notice how Box G and Box I differ:

- $a - 3 = -6$
- $3 - a = -6$

Not only do the two equations have different solutions, but one is harder to solve than the other **(the second equation involves a hidden negative coefficient in front of the variable).**

This lesson focuses on these little details that can have a big impact on the solution.

Lesson 3: One-Step Equations

Part 1: Solve.

A.	B. Find the inverse.	C.	D.
$5 + 7 = 12$	$7 - 7 = 0$	$5 \cdot 7 = 35$	$\frac{1}{7} \cdot 7 = 1$
$5 + -7 = -2$	$-9 + 9 = 0$	$5 \cdot -7 = -35$	E.
$-5 + 7 = 2$	$5 - 5 = 0$	$-5 \cdot 7 = -35$	$\frac{-7}{-7} = 1$
$-5 + -7 = -12$	$-5 + 5 = 0$	$-5 \cdot -7 = 35$	

Part 2: Solve. Notice and focus on the subtle differences between the problems in each row.

F. $b + 7 = 42$ → $b = 35$
G. $b - 7 = 42$ → $b = 49$
H. $7 + b = -42$ → $b = -49$
I. $-7 - b = -42$ → $-b = -35$ → $b = 35$ (Careful! Hidden negative coefficient.)

J. $\frac{7b}{7} = \frac{42}{7}$ → $b = 6$
K. $\frac{7b}{-7} = \frac{-42}{-7}$ → $b = 6$
L. $\frac{-42}{-7} = \frac{7b}{-7}$ → $b = -6$
M. $\frac{42}{7} = \frac{7b}{7}$ → $b = 6$

N. $\frac{-7b}{-7} = \frac{42}{-7}$ → $b = -6$
O. $\frac{7b}{7} = \frac{-42}{7}$ → $b = -6$
P. $\frac{-42}{-7} = \frac{7b}{-7}$ → $b = 6$
Q. $\frac{42}{7} = \frac{-7b}{7}$ → $b = -6$

R. $7 \cdot \frac{b}{7} = 42 \cdot 7$ → $b = 294$
S. $7 \cdot 42 = \frac{b}{7} \cdot 7$ → $b = 294$
T. $10 \cdot \frac{b}{10} = 12 \cdot 10$ → $b = 120$
U. $11 \cdot 12 = \frac{b}{11} \cdot 11$ → $b = 132$

Key Points from Demo Video – Lesson 3
One-Step Equations

Lesson 3 builds upon Lessons 1 and 2. Even one-step equations can be tricky because a single step can involve one of many possibilities:

- add, subtract, multiply, or divide
- positive or negative values
- variable on the left or right of the equal sign

Part 1 reviews prerequisite skills, including adding, subtracting, multiplying, and dividing integers.

In Part 2, students solve each equation, as shown in the demo video. **Notice and focus on the subtle differences between the problems.** For example, notice how Box J and Box O differ:

- $7b = 42$
- $7b = -42$

This lesson focuses on these little details that can have a big impact on the solution.

Lesson 4: Setting Up and Solving One-Step Equations

KEY LESSON

Directions: Follow along with your instructor to complete this lesson. Set up and solve the equations for the word problems below. Draw a bar model to check your work.

A. A number equals 42.
$n = 42$
Bar Model: 42 | 42

B. Seven added to a number equals 42.
$n + 7 = 42$ → $n = 35$
Bar Model: 42 | 35, 7

C. Seven subtracted from a number is 42.
$n - 7 = 42$ → $n = 49$
Bar Model: 49 | 42, 7

D. A number multiplied by 7 equals 42.
$\frac{7n}{7} = \frac{42}{7}$ → $n = 6$
Bar Model: 42 | 6 6 6 6 6 6 6

E. A number doubled equals 16.
$\frac{2n}{2} = \frac{16}{2}$ → $n = 8$
Bar Model: 16 | 8 8

F. Half of a number equals 16.
$2 \cdot \frac{n}{2} = 16 \cdot 2$ → $n = 32$
Bar Model: 32 | 16 16

G. One third of a number is 21.
$3 \cdot \frac{n}{3} = 21 \cdot 3$ → $n = 63$
Bar Model: 63 | 21 21 21

H. Two thirds of a number is 8.
$\frac{3}{2} \cdot \frac{2}{3} n = 8 \cdot \frac{3}{2}$ → $n = 12$
Bar Model: 8 | 4 4 | 4 / 12

I. Three fourths of a number is 15.
$\frac{4}{3} \cdot \frac{3}{4} n = 15 \cdot \frac{4}{3}$ → $n = 20$
Bar Model: 15 | 5 5 5 | 5 / 20

Key Points from Demo Video – Lesson 4
Setting Up and Solving One-Step Equations

In Lesson 4, students follow along with their instructor to set up and solve equations, as shown in the demo video.

As in the previous lessons, this lesson focuses on little variations that students must pay attention to since those little details can have a big impact on the solution. For example, notice the differences between Box B and Box C:

- Seven added to a number equals 42.
- Seven subtracted from a number equals 42.

That one little difference (added to vs. subtracted from) results in two completely different solutions for Box B and Box C (35 vs. 49).

In addition to setting up and solving each equation, students follow along with their instructor to draw a **bar model** of each situation. The demo video shows how to draw each bar model.

Boxes F, G, H, and I involve fractions. Box F and Box G are easier to solve because they involve unit fractions (1/2 and 1/3) where the numerator is 1. Box H and Box I are more challenging.

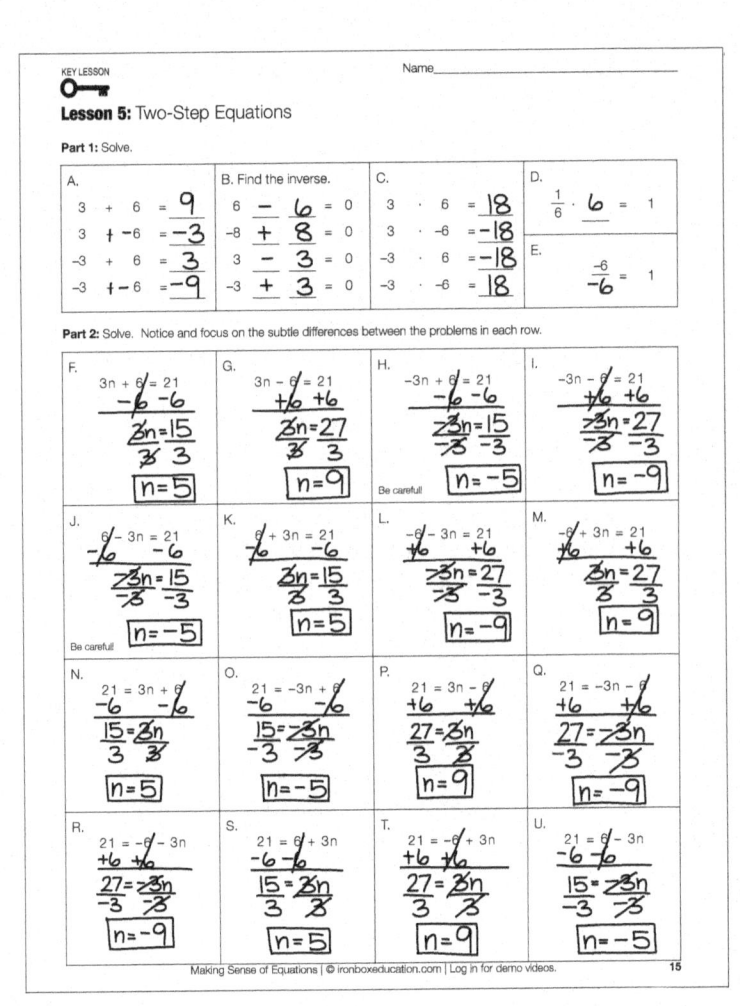

Lesson 5: Two-Step Equations

Part 1: Solve.

A.	B. Find the inverse.	C.	D.
$3 + 6 = 9$	$6 - 6 = 0$	$3 \cdot 6 = 18$	$\frac{1}{6} \cdot 6 = 1$
$3 + -6 = -3$	$-8 + 8 = 0$	$3 \cdot -6 = -18$	E.
$-3 + 6 = 3$	$3 - 3 = 0$	$-3 \cdot 6 = -18$	$\frac{-6}{-6} = 1$
$-3 + -6 = -9$	$-3 + 3 = 0$	$-3 \cdot -6 = 18$	

Part 2: Solve. Notice and focus on the subtle differences between the problems in each row.

F. $3n + 6 = 21$; $3n = 15$; $n = 5$
G. $3n - 6 = 21$; $3n = 27$; $n = 9$
H. $-3n + 6 = 21$; $-3n = 15$; $n = -5$ (Be careful)
I. $-3n - 6 = 21$; $-3n = 27$; $n = -9$

J. $6 - 3n = 21$; $-3n = 15$; $n = -5$ (Be careful)
K. $6 + 3n = 21$; $3n = 15$; $n = 5$
L. $-6 - 3n = 21$; $-3n = 27$; $n = -9$
M. $-6 + 3n = 21$; $3n = 27$; $n = 9$

N. $21 = 3n + 6$; $15 = 3n$; $n = 5$
O. $21 = -3n + 6$; $15 = -3n$; $n = -5$
P. $21 = 3n - 6$; $27 = 3n$; $n = 9$
Q. $21 = -3n - 6$; $27 = -3n$; $n = -9$

R. $21 = 6 - 3n$; $27 = -3n$; $n = -9$
S. $21 = 6 + 3n$; $15 = 3n$; $n = 5$
T. $21 = -6 + 3n$; $27 = 3n$; $n = 9$
U. $21 = -6 - 3n$; $15 = -3n$; $n = -5$

Key Points from Demo Video – Lesson 5
Two-Step Equations

As was shown in Lessons 1-3, even one-step equations can be tricky because a single step can involve one of many possibilities.

Now, Lesson 5 takes it to the next level with two-step equations.

Again, students must pay close attention to the subtle differences between problems. The equations look similar, but they have very different solutions.

These two-step equations involve two operations – multiplication and either addition or subtraction.

- First, a variable n is multiplied.
- Then it is either added to or subtracted from a number (or vice versa).

To isolate the variable n, work your way backwards.

- Undo addition by using subtraction (or undo subtraction by using addition).
- Then, undo multiplication by using division.

Students should box their final answers for better visibility.

Lesson 6: Two-Step Equations

Part 1: Solve.

A.	B. Find the inverse.	C.	D.
$4 + 3 = 7$	$3 - 3 = 0$	$3 \cdot 3 = 9$	$\frac{1}{4} \cdot 4 = 1$
$4 - 3 = 1$	$-5 + 5 = 0$	$3 \cdot -3 = -9$	E.
$-4 + 3 = -1$	$4 - 4 = 0$	$-4 \cdot 3 = -12$	$\frac{-4}{-4} = 1$
$-4 - 3 = -7$	$-4 + 4 = 0$	$-4 \cdot -3 = 12$	

Part 2: Solve. Notice and focus on the subtle differences between the problems in each row.

F. **NEW TYPE OF PROBLEM** $3(y + 2) = 18$; $y + 2 = 6$; $y = 4$
G. $3(y - 2) = 18$; $y - 2 = 6$; $y = 8$
H. $-3(y + 2) = -18$; $y + 2 = 6$; $y = 4$
I. $-3(y - 2) = -18$; $y - 2 = 6$; $y = 8$

J. $-9 - 3y = -6$; $-3y = 3$; $y = -1$ ... (partial)
K. $-9 + 3y = -6$; $3y = 3$; $y = 1$
L. $-9 - 3y = -6$
M. $-9 + 3y = -6$

N. $-6 = 2(y + 9)$; $-3 = y + 9$; $-12 = y$
O. $-6 = -2(y + 9)$; $3 = y + 9$; $-6 = y$
P. $-6 = 2(y - 9)$; $-3 = y - 9$; $6 = y$
Q. $-6 = -2(y - 9)$; $3 = y - 9$; $12 = y$

R. $-6 = -9 - 3y$; $3 = -3y$; $-1 = y$
S. $-6 = -9 + 3y$; $3 = 3y$; $1 = y$
T. $-6 = -9 + 3y$
U. $-6 = -9 - 3y$; $15 = -3y$; $5 = y$

Key Points from Demo Video – Lesson 6
Two-Step Equations

Lesson 6 builds upon the two-step equations introduced in Lesson 5.

Pay close attention to the subtle differences between problems. The equations look similar, but they have very different solutions.

Again, these two-step equations involve two operations. However, **a new type of problem** is introduced:

- First, a number is added to or subtracted from a variable.
- Then, that sum or difference is multiplied.

To isolate the variable n from these types of problems work your way backwards in this manner:

- Undo multiplication by using division.
- Then, undo addition by using subtraction (or undo subtraction by using addition).

Students should box their final answers for better visibility.

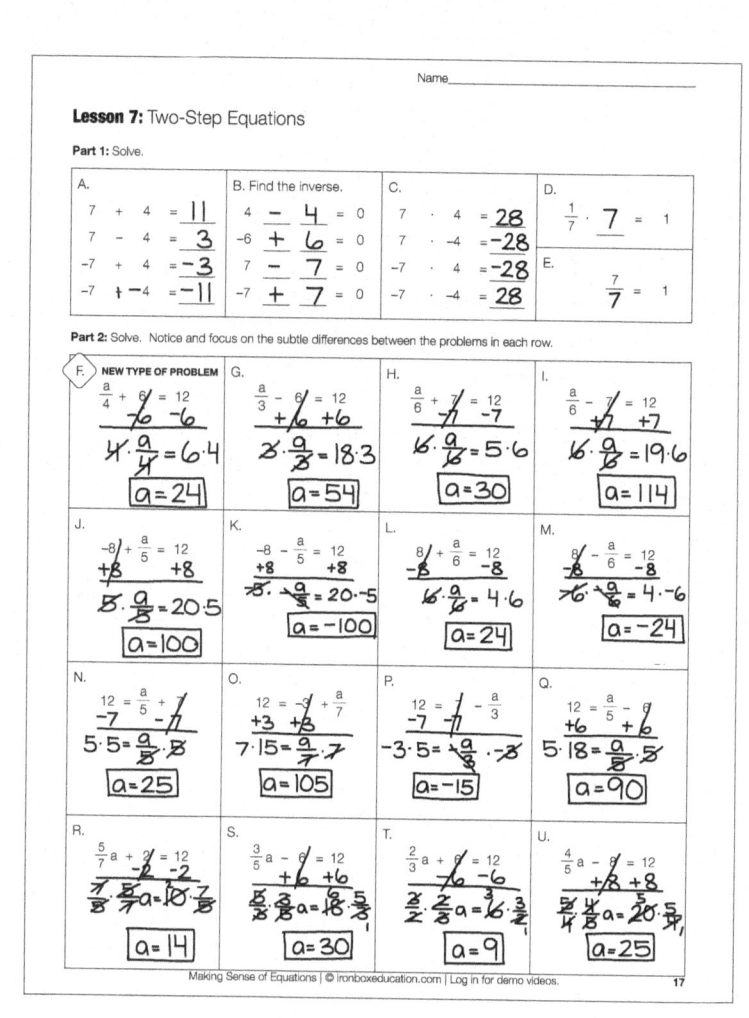

Key Points from Demo Video – Lesson 7
Two-Step Equations

Lesson 7 builds upon the two-step equations introduced in Lessons 5 and 6, and it introduces **a third type of problem:**

- First, a variable is divided by a number.
- Then, another number is added to or subtracted from the quotient (or vice versa).

To isolate the variable n from these types of problems work your way backwards in this manner:

- Undo addition by using subtraction (or undo subtraction by using addition).
- Then, undo division by using multiplication.

Box final answers for better visibility.

Key Points from Demo Video – Lesson 8
Two-Step Equations

Lesson 8 builds upon the two-step equations introduced in Lessons 5, 6 and 7, and it introduces **a fourth type of problem:**

- First, a number is added to or subtracted from a variable.
- Then, the sum or difference is divided.

To isolate the variable n from these types of problems work your way backwards in this manner:

- Undo division by using multiplication.
- Then, undo addition by using subtraction (or undo subtraction by using addition).

Box final answers for better visibility.

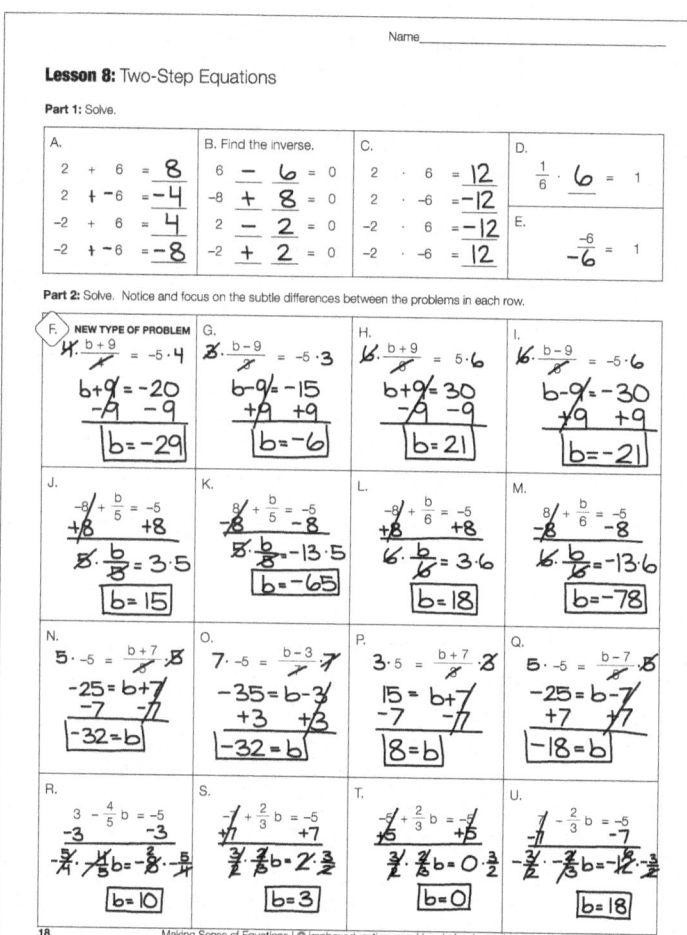

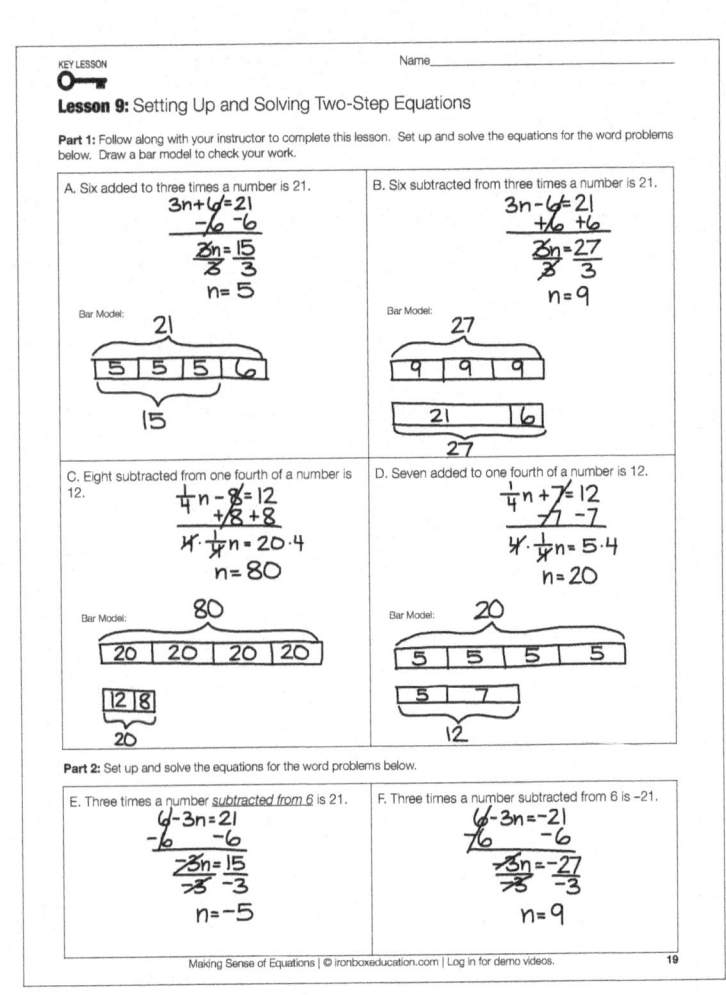

Key Points from Demo Video – Lesson 9
Setting Up and Solving Two-Step Equations

In Lesson 4, students set up and solved one-step equations.

In Lesson 9, students follow along with their instructor to set up and solve two-step equations, as shown in the demo video.

As in the previous lessons, **this lesson focuses on little variations that students must pay attention to since those little details can have a big impact on the solution.**

In Part 1, in addition to setting up and solving each equation, students follow along with their instructor to draw a **bar model** of each situation. The demo video shows how to draw each bar model.

In Part 2, students set up and solve equations without using a bar model.

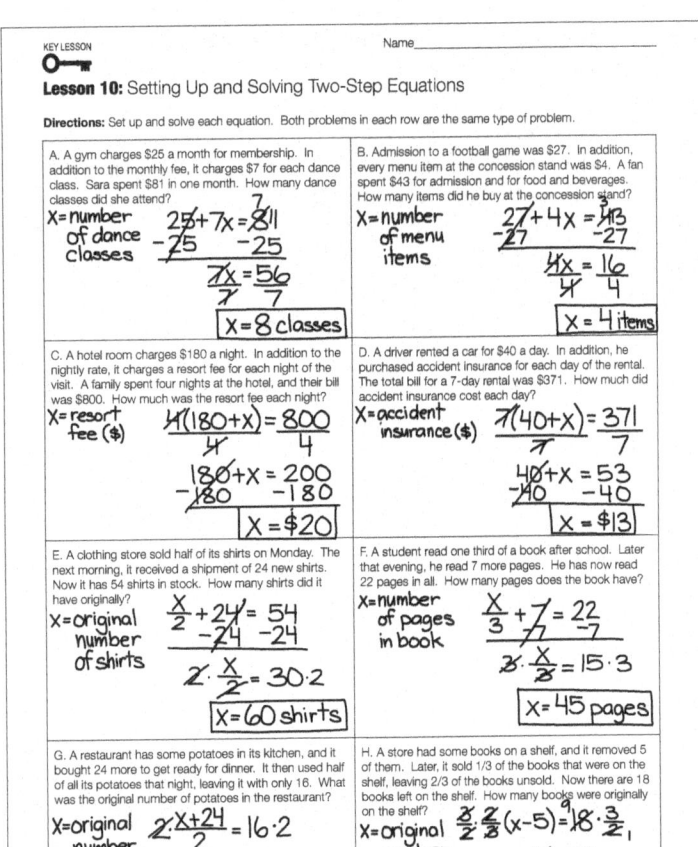

Lesson 9: Setting Up and Solving Two-Step Equations

Part 1: Follow along with your instructor to complete this lesson. Set up and solve the equations for the word problems below. Draw a bar model to check your work.

A. Six added to three times a number is 21.
$$3n + 6 = 21$$
$$-6 \quad -6$$
$$\frac{3n}{3} = \frac{15}{3}$$
$$n = 5$$

B. Six subtracted from three times a number is 21.
$$3n - 6 = 21$$
$$+6 \quad +6$$
$$\frac{3n}{3} = \frac{27}{3}$$
$$n = 9$$

C. Eight subtracted from one fourth of a number is 12.
$$\tfrac{1}{4}n - 8 = 12$$
$$+8 \quad +8$$
$$4 \cdot \tfrac{1}{4}n = 20 \cdot 4$$
$$n = 80$$

D. Seven added to one fourth of a number is 12.
$$\tfrac{1}{4}n + 7 = 12$$
$$-7 \quad -7$$
$$4 \cdot \tfrac{1}{4}n = 5 \cdot 4$$
$$n = 20$$

Part 2: Set up and solve the equations for the word problems below.

E. Three times a number *subtracted from 6* is 21.
$$6 - 3n = 21$$
$$-6 \quad -6$$
$$\frac{-3n}{-3} = \frac{15}{-3}$$
$$n = -5$$

F. Three times a number subtracted from 6 is –21.
$$6 - 3n = -21$$
$$-6 \quad -6$$
$$\frac{-3n}{-3} = \frac{-27}{-3}$$
$$n = 9$$

Key Points from Demo Video – Lesson 10
Setting Up and Solving Two-Step Equations

In Lesson 10, students continue setting up and solving two-step equations.

For each problem, set up the variable before setting up each equation. For example, the setup for the variable in Box A is:

- x = number of dance classes

After solving the equation, include the units in the answer. The solution in Box A is:

- x = 8 classes

and not just x = 8.

Both problems in each row are the same type of problem:

1. A variable multiplied is added to a number.
2. A variable is added to a number, then the sum is multiplied.
3. A number is added to a fraction of a variable.
4. A number is added to a variable, then a fraction of the sum is found.

Lesson 10: Setting Up and Solving Two-Step Equations

Directions: Set up and solve each equation. Both problems in each row are the same type of problem.

A. A gym charges $25 a month for membership. In addition to the monthly fee, it charges $7 for each dance class. Sara spent $81 in one month. How many dance classes did she attend?
x = number of dance classes
$$25 + 7x = 81$$
$$-25 \quad -25$$
$$\frac{7x}{7} = \frac{56}{7}$$
$$\boxed{x = 8 \text{ classes}}$$

B. Admission to a football game was $27. In addition, every menu item at the concession stand was $4. A fan spent $43 for admission and for food and beverages. How many items did he buy at the concession stand?
x = number of menu items
$$27 + 4x = 43$$
$$-27 \quad -27$$
$$\frac{4x}{4} = \frac{16}{4}$$
$$\boxed{x = 4 \text{ items}}$$

C. A hotel room charges $180 a night. In addition to the nightly rate, it charges a resort fee for each night of the visit. A family spent four nights at the hotel, and their bill was $800. How much was the resort fee each night?
x = resort fee ($)
$$\frac{4(180+x)}{4} = \frac{800}{4}$$
$$180 + x = 200$$
$$-180 \quad -180$$
$$\boxed{x = \$20}$$

D. A driver rented a car for $40 a day. In addition, he purchased accident insurance for each day of the rental. The total bill for a 7-day rental was $371. How much did accident insurance cost each day?
x = accident insurance ($)
$$\frac{7(40+x)}{7} = \frac{371}{7}$$
$$40 + x = 53$$
$$-40 \quad -40$$
$$\boxed{x = \$13}$$

E. A clothing store sold half of its shirts on Monday. The next morning, it received a shipment of 24 new shirts. Now it has 54 shirts in stock. How many shirts did it have originally?
x = original number of shirts
$$\tfrac{x}{2} + 24 = 54$$
$$-24 \quad -24$$
$$2 \cdot \tfrac{x}{2} = 30 \cdot 2$$
$$\boxed{x = 60 \text{ shirts}}$$

F. A student read one third of a book after school. Later that evening, he read 7 more pages. He has now read 22 pages in all. How many pages does the book have?
x = number of pages in book
$$\tfrac{x}{3} + 7 = 22$$
$$-7 \quad -7$$
$$3 \cdot \tfrac{x}{3} = 15 \cdot 3$$
$$\boxed{x = 45 \text{ pages}}$$

G. A restaurant has some potatoes in its kitchen, and it bought 24 more to get ready for dinner. It then used half of all its potatoes that night, leaving it with only 16. What was the original number of potatoes in the restaurant?
x = original number of potatoes
$$2 \cdot \tfrac{x+24}{2} = 16 \cdot 2$$
$$x + 24 = 32$$
$$-24 \quad -24$$
$$\boxed{x = 8 \text{ potatoes}}$$

H. A store had some books on a shelf and it removed 5 of them. Later, it sold 1/3 of the books that were on the shelf, leaving 2/3 of the books unsold. Now there are 18 books left on the shelf. How many books were originally on the shelf?
x = original number of books
$$\tfrac{3}{2} \cdot \tfrac{2}{3}(x-5) = 18 \cdot \tfrac{3}{2}$$
$$x - 5 = 27$$
$$+5 \quad +5$$
$$\boxed{x = 32 \text{ books}}$$

Lesson 11: Setting Up and Solving Two-Step Equations

Directions: Set up and solve each equation. Both problems in each row are the same type of problem.

A. Jennifer started her trip with $84. She bought 3 bottles of water, and now she has $72.75 left. How much did each bottle of water cost? x = cost of bottle ($) $84 - 3x = 72.75$ $-84 \quad -84.00$ $\dfrac{-3x}{-3} = \dfrac{-11.25}{-3}$ $3\overline{)11.25} = 3.75$ $\boxed{x = \$3.75}$	**B.** To rent a bike at the beach, it costs $15 upfront, plus an additional $7 per hour. How many hours was a bike rented if the total cost was $36? x = number of hours $15 + 7x = 36$ $-15 \quad -15$ $\dfrac{7x}{7} = \dfrac{21}{7}$ $\boxed{x = 3\text{ hours}}$
C. A plane ticket costs $220. In addition to the airfare, each passenger must pay a landing fee. A family of three paid $714. How much is the landing fee per passenger? x = landing fee ($) $\dfrac{3(220+x)}{3} = \dfrac{714}{3}$ $3\overline{)714} = 238$ $220 + x = 238$ $-220 \quad -220$ $\boxed{x = \$18}$	**D.** Every book ordered from an online store costs $12. In addition, the customer pays a shipping charge for every book. A customer purchases 5 books, spending $80. How much is the shipping charge for each book? x = shipping charge ($) $\dfrac{5(12+x)}{5} = \dfrac{80}{5}$ $5\overline{)80} = 16$ $12 + x = 16$ $-12 \quad -12$ $\boxed{x = \$4}$
E. An airplane completed three fifths of its flight before noon. A short while later, it traveled an additional 125 miles, for a total of 1,625 miles. How many miles long was the total flight? x = length of flight (miles) $\tfrac{3}{5}x + 125 = 1625$ $-125 \quad -125$ $\tfrac{5}{3} \cdot \tfrac{3}{5}x = 1500 \cdot \tfrac{5}{3}$ $\boxed{x = 2{,}500\text{ miles}}$	**F.** A bird ate 3/4 of the food in her dish, leaving only 1/4 of her food in the dish. Later, her owner added 17 grams of food to the dish, bringing the total to 26 grams. What was the original amount of food in the dish? x = original grams of food $\tfrac{1}{4}x + 17 = 26$ $-17 \quad -17$ $4 \cdot \tfrac{1}{4}x = 9 \cdot 4$ $\boxed{x = 36\text{ grams}}$
G. John started with $21. Then, he received some money for his allowance. Later, he spent 2/3 of all his money on a toy, leaving him with 1/3 of his money. Now he has $9. How much did he receive for his allowance? x = allowance ($) $3 \cdot \dfrac{(21+x)}{3} = 9 \cdot 3$ $21 + x = 27$ $-21 \quad -21$ $\boxed{x = \$6}$	**H.** A cooler had 42 cups of water in it. A team's coach added another 16 cups. The team then drank half of the water in the cooler. How much water was left in the cooler? x = cups of water left in cooler $\dfrac{(42+16)}{2} = x$ $\dfrac{58}{2} = x$ $\boxed{x = 29\text{ cups}}$

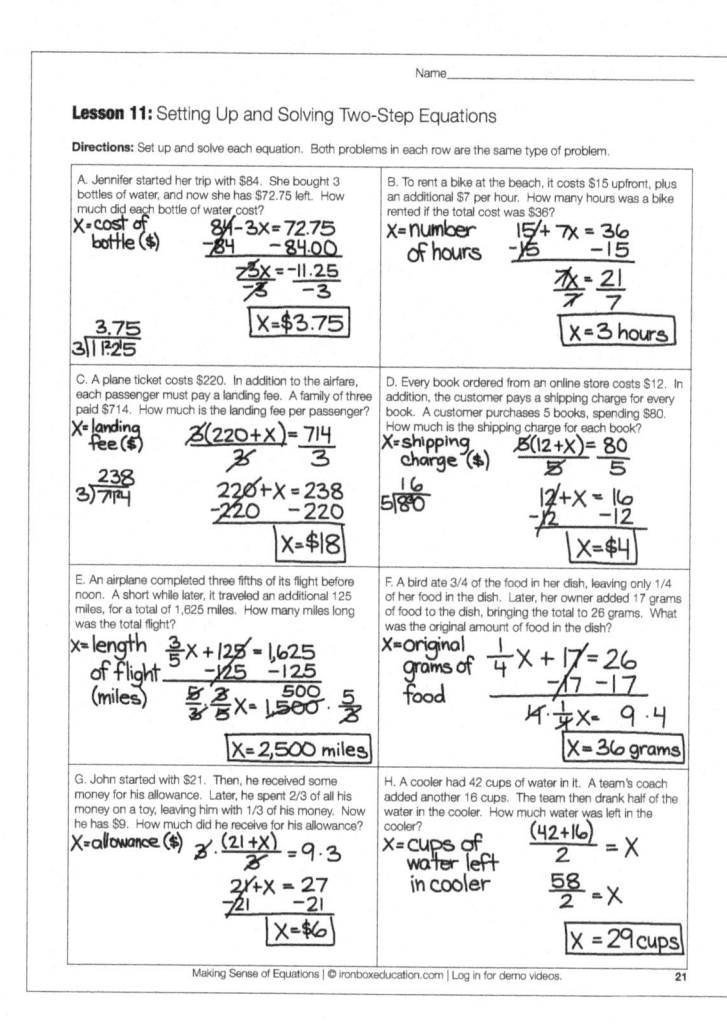

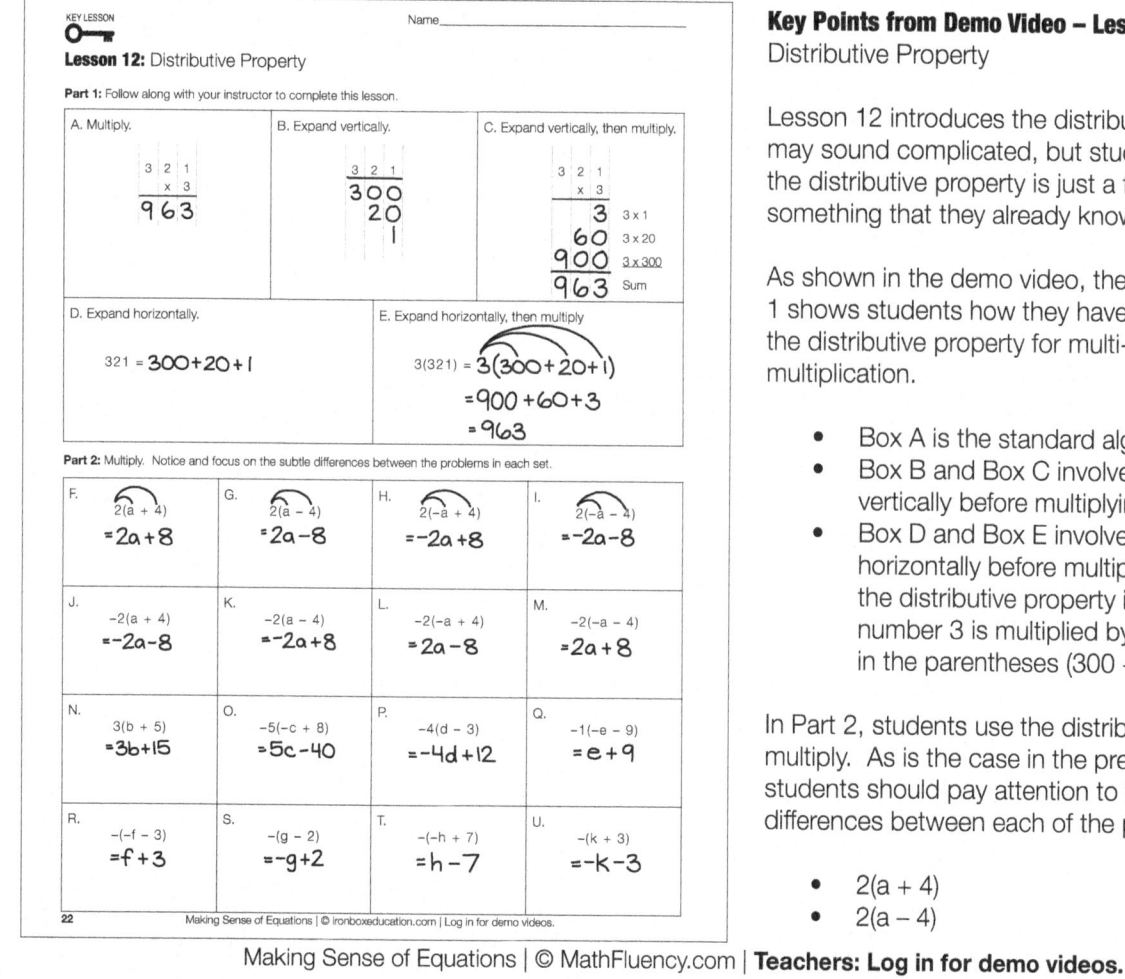

Key Points from Demo Video – Lesson 11
Setting Up and Solving Two-Step Equations

In Lesson 11, students continue setting up and solving two-step equations. For each problem, set up the variable before setting up each equation. For example, the setup for the variable in Box A is:

- x = cost of bottle ($)

After solving the equation, include the units in the answer. The solution in Box A is:

- x = $3.75

and not just x = 3.75.

The types of problems found in this lesson include the following:

1. A variable multiplied is added to (or subtracted from) a number.
2. A variable is added to a number, then the sum is multiplied.
3. A number is added to a fraction of a variable.
4. A variable is added to a number, then a fraction of the sum is found.

KEY LESSON

Lesson 12: Distributive Property

Part 1: Follow along with your instructor to complete this lesson.

A. Multiply.	B. Expand vertically.	C. Expand vertically, then multiply.

3 2 1
×   3
────
9 6 3
	3 2 1
	────
	3 0 0
	 2 0
	   1
		3 2 1
		× 3
		────
		   3 3 × 1
		 6 0 3 × 20
		9 0 0 3 × 300
		────
		9 6 3 Sum

D. Expand horizontally.	E. Expand horizontally, then multiply
$321 = 300 + 20 + 1$	$3(321) = 3(300 + 20 + 1)$ $= 900 + 60 + 3$ $= 963$

Part 2: Multiply. Notice and focus on the subtle differences between the problems in each set.

F. $2(a+4)$ $= 2a + 8$	G. $2(a-4)$ $= 2a - 8$	H. $2(-a+4)$ $= -2a + 8$	I. $2(-a-4)$ $= -2a - 8$
J. $-2(a+4)$ $= -2a - 8$	K. $-2(a-4)$ $= -2a + 8$	L. $-2(-a+4)$ $= 2a - 8$	M. $-2(-a-4)$ $= 2a + 8$
N. $3(b+5)$ $= 3b + 15$	O. $-5(-c+8)$ $= 5c - 40$	P. $-4(d-3)$ $= -4d + 12$	Q. $-1(-e-9)$ $= e + 9$
R. $-(-f-3)$ $= f + 3$	S. $-(g-2)$ $= -g + 2$	T. $-(-h+7)$ $= h - 7$	U. $-(k+3)$ $= -k - 3$

Key Points from Demo Video – Lesson 12
Distributive Property

Lesson 12 introduces the distributive property. It may sound complicated, but students will see that the distributive property is just a fancy term for something that they already know how to use.

As shown in the demo video, the progression in Part 1 shows students how they have already been using the distributive property for multi-digit by single-digit multiplication.

- Box A is the standard algorithm.
- Box B and Box C involve expanding 321 vertically before multiplying.
- Box D and Box E involve expanding 321 horizontally before multiplying. Box E shows the distributive property in practice. The number 3 is multiplied by each of the terms in the parentheses (300 + 20 + 1).

In Part 2, students use the distributive property to multiply. As is the case in the previous lessons, students should pay attention to the subtle differences between each of the problems, such as:

- 2(a + 4)
- 2(a − 4)

Lesson 13: Distributive Property

Part 1: Use the distributive property to multiply. Write your negative signs clearly.

A. $a(b+c)$ $= ab+ac$	B. $a(-b+c)$ $= -ab+ac$	C. $-a(b+c)$ $= -ab-ac$	D. $-a(-b+c)$ $= ab-ac$
E. $a(b-c)$ $= ab-ac$	F. $a(-b-c)$ $= -ab-ac$	G. $-a(b-c)$ $= -ab+ac$	H. $-a(-b-c)$ $= ab+ac$

Part 2: Use the distributive property to multiply. Write your negative signs clearly.

I. $2(3a+1)$ $= 6a+2$	J. $-3(-5e-8)$ $= 15e+24$	K. $-3a(2a-3b+c)$ $= -6a^2+9ab-3ac$
L. $-1(-5b+4)$ $= 5b-4$	M. $-(3a-c+6)$ $= -3a+c-6$	N. $-5a(2a-5b-2c)$ $= -10a^2+25ab+10ac$
O. $-5(6c-5)$ $= -30c+25$	P. $8(-6g+3)$ $= -48g+24$	Q. $-a(-9a^2-3a)$ $= 9a^3+3a^2$
R. $-(-9d^2-2d)$ $= 9d^2+2d$	S. $-6h(3h^2+7h)$ $= -18h^3-42h^2$	T. $-5a(-6a^3-2a^2+a)$ $= 30a^4+10a^3-5a^2$

Key Points from Demo Video – Lesson 13
Distributive Property

In Lesson 13, students practice using the distributive property, which they learned in Lesson 12.

In Part 1, each of the problems uses the variables *a*, *b*, and *c*. The only differences between the problems involve the following:

- the use of positive or negative signs
- addition or subtraction symbols inside the parentheses

Students must pay especially close attention to these details.

In Part 2, students use the distributive property to multiply. For several of the problems, students need to use the rule for multiplying exponents that they learned in *Making Sense of Exponents*:

- $x^a \cdot x^b = x^{(a+b)}$

Example:

$x \cdot x^3$
$= x^1 \cdot x^3$
$= x^4$

KEY LESSON
Lesson 14: Factoring

Part 1: Simplify using the GCF (Greatest Common Factor). Remember to ask the Magic Question first.

A. GCF=2 $\frac{8 \div 2}{10 \div 2} = \frac{4}{5}$	B. GCF=5 $\frac{10 \div 5}{25 \div 5} = \frac{2}{5}$	C. $\frac{5 \div 5}{25 \div 5} = \frac{1}{5}$	D. $\frac{6 \div 3}{21 \div 3} = \frac{2}{7}$	E. $\frac{4 \div 4}{16 \div 4} = \frac{1}{4}$
F. $\frac{12 \div 4}{16 \div 4} = \frac{3}{4}$	G. $\frac{18 \div 6}{30 \div 6} = \frac{3}{5}$	H. $\frac{12}{12} = 1$	I. $\frac{3 \div 3}{15 \div 3} = \frac{1}{5}$	J. $\frac{20}{20} = 1$

Part 2: Factor each expression. Then, multiply the factors to check your work.

K. GCF=2 $8x+10y$ $=2(4x+5y)$ Factor.	$2(4x+5y)$ $=8x+10y$ ✓ Multiply to check.	L. GCF=5 $10x-25y$ $=5(2x-5y)$ Factor.	$5(2x-5y)$ $=10x-25y$ ✓ Multiply to check.

Part 3: Factor each expression.

M. $5a+25b$ $=5(a+5b)$	N. $3c+15d$ $=3(c+5d)$	O. $12e+16f$ $=4(3e+4f)$	P. $20x+20y+20z$ $=20(x+y+z)$
Q. $4m-16n$ $=4(m-4n)$ Careful: Negative values.	R. $-12r-12s$ $=-12(r+s)$ Hint: Factor out -12.	S. $-6t-9u$ $=-3(2t+3u)$ Hint: Factor out a negative value.	T. $18v-30w$ $=6(3v-5w)$

Part 4: Follow along with your instructor to factor each expression. Use the extra white space as scratch paper.

U. $7a+49ab$ $=7a(1+7b)$	V. $10x-25xy$ $=5x(2-5y)$	W. $8c^2-64c$ $=8c(c-8)$	X. $9x^3+81x^2$ $=9x^2(x+9)$
$\frac{7a+49ab}{7a}$	$\frac{10x-25xy}{5x}$	$\frac{8c^2-64c}{8c}$	$\frac{9x^3+81x^2}{9x^2}$

Key Points from Demo Video – Lesson 14
Factoring

As shown in the demo video, factoring reverses the distributive property.

In Part 1, students review using the GCF (Greatest Common Factor) to simplify fractions.

Box A shows 8/10 being simplified by dividing the numerator and the denominator by the GCF of 2.

$\frac{8 \div 2}{10 \div 2} = \frac{4}{5}$

Similarly, Box K shows the product 8x + 10y, which also has a GCF of 2. Factoring out the 2 gives you:

$8x + 10y$
$=2(4x+5y)$

To verify, multiply the factors of **2** and **(4x + 5y)**.

$2(4x+5y)$
$=8x+10y$ ✓

In Part 4, use the white space as scratch paper to more easily find the GCF to make it easier to factor.

Lesson 15: Order of Operations

Part 1: Follow along with your instructor to complete this lesson.

The expressions in Box A and Box B use the same numbers of __2__, __5__, and __3__. They also use the same operations of __addition__ and __multiplication__. The __parentheses__ tell us which operation to perform first.

- In Box A, the parentheses tell us to perform the __addition__ operation first.
- In Box B, the parentheses tell us to perform the __multiplication__ operation first.

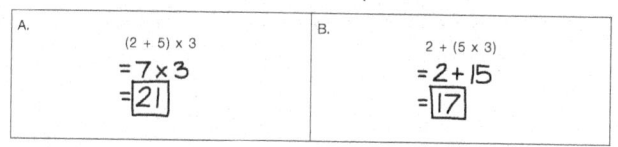

A.	B.
$(2 + 5) \times 3$ $= 7 \times 3$ $= \boxed{21}$	$2 + (5 \times 3)$ $= 2 + 15$ $= \boxed{17}$

Even though Box A and Box B used the same numbers and the same operations, they each gave us different __values__. This shows that the order of operations __matters__. To prevent __confusion__ and to make sure everyone gets the same value when simplifying expressions and equations, we use the following __order of operations__.

- First, perform the operations inside the __parentheses__ or other grouping symbols.
- Then, simplify __exponents__ and roots.
- Next, simplify both __multiplication__ and __division__ from left to right.
- Finally, simplify both __addition__ and __subtraction__ from left to right.

Use the common acronym __P E MD AS__ to remember the order of operations.

Part 2: Simplify each expression using the order of operations.

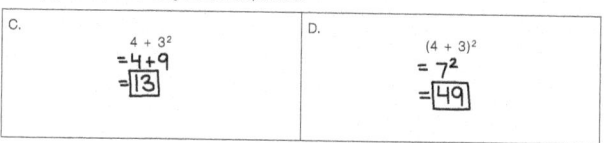

C.	D.
$4 + 3^2$ $= 4 + 9$ $= \boxed{13}$	$(4 + 3)^2$ $= 7^2$ $= \boxed{49}$

Key Points from Demo Video – Lesson 15
Order of Operations

Lesson 15 shows that the order of operations matters.

In Part 1, the expressions in Box A and Box B use the same numbers of 2, 5, and 3. They also use the same operations of addition and multiplication. Only the order of operations is different.

- Box A (addition first) gives us 21.
- Box B (multiplication first) gives us 17.

This shows that the order of operations matters. There is an agreed-upon order of operations that prevents confusion and makes sure that everyone arrives at the same value when simplifying the same expressions and equations:

- First, perform the operations inside the Parentheses or other grouping symbols.
- Then, simplify Exponents and roots.
- Next, simplify both Multiplication and Division from left to right.
- Finally, simplify both Addition and Subtraction from left to right.

This is summarized using the acronym P E MD AS.

Lesson 16: Order of Operations

Part 1: Simplify each expression using the order of operations (P E MD AS).

A.	B.
$6 + (3 \times 4 \div 2) - 1$ $= 6 + 6 - 1$ $= \boxed{11}$	$6 + 3 \times 4 \div (2 - 1)$ $= 6 + (3 \times 4 \div 1)$ $= 6 + 12$ $= \boxed{18}$
C.	D.
$(6 + 3 \times 4) \div 2 - 1$ $= (6 + 12) \div 2 - 1$ $= 18 \div 2 - 1$ $= 9 - 1 = \boxed{8}$	$6 + 3 \times (4 \div 2 - 1)$ $= 6 + 3 \times (2 - 1)$ $= 6 + 3 \times 1$ $= 6 + 3 = \boxed{9}$

Part 2: This next set of problems uses only multiplication, division, addition, and subtraction. Remember that **multiplication and division** take precedence over **addition and subtraction**. To make this easier to see, use parentheses to group together numbers that are being multiplied or divided. Then, simplify.

Example:
$5 + 6 \div 2 + 3 \times 4 \div 2$
$= 5 + (6 \div 2) + (3 \times 4 \div 2)$
$= 5 + 3 + 6$
$= 14$

E.	F.
$(8 \div 2) + (9 \times 3 \times 2) - 10$ $= 4 + 6 - 10$ $= \boxed{0}$	$3 + (5 \times 3) - (10 \div 2 \times 3)$ $= 3 + 15 - 15$ $= \boxed{3}$
G.	H.
$(4 \times 5) - (6 \times 3) + (8 \div 4)$ $= 20 - 18 + 2$ $= \boxed{4}$	$9 - (14 \div 2) + 4 + (5 \times 2)$ $= 9 - 7 + 4 + 10$ $= \boxed{16}$
I.	J.
$8 - (4 \div 2) + 6 + (2 \times 4)$ $= 8 - 2 + 6 + 8$ $= \boxed{20}$	$5 - (9 \div 3) + (12 \div 6 \times 2)$ $= 5 - 3 + 4$ $= \boxed{6}$

Key Points from Demo Video – Lesson 16
Order of Operations

The previous lesson showed that the order of operations matters. In Lesson 16, students practice using the order of operations.

In Part 1, simplify each expression using the order of operations (P E MD AS).

Remember that multiplication and division take precedence over addition and subtraction.

To make this easier to see in Box A, students can add parentheses to 6 + **3 x 4 ÷ 2** – 1 and rewrite it as 6 + (3 x 4 ÷ 2) – 1.

This makes it more clear that students should perform both multiplication and division operations first from left to right before performing both addition and subtraction operations next from left to right.

Add parentheses in the same way to all the problems in Part 2.

Key Points from Demo Video – Lesson 17
Order of Operations

In Lesson 17, students continue working with order of operations, and the complexity level increases.

Part 1 involves exponents and nested parentheses (parentheses within parentheses). Also, Box C and Box D involve division operations written in the form of fractions.

Part 2 involves fractions and negative values. Students should use parentheses to show that multiplication and division take precedence over addition and subtraction.

In Box E, for example, $1 \div 10 + 3 \div 10 + 5 \div 10$ should be written as $(1 \div 10) + (3 \div 10) + (5 \div 10)$. This results in the following:

$$\frac{1}{10} + \frac{3}{10} + \frac{5}{10} = \boxed{\frac{9}{10}}$$

Box F, Box G, and Box I result in negative values.

Box H and Box J result in mixed numbers.

Lesson 17: Order of Operations

Part 1: Simplify each expression using the order of operations (P E MD AS). Some of these problems involve exponents and nested parentheses (parentheses within parentheses).

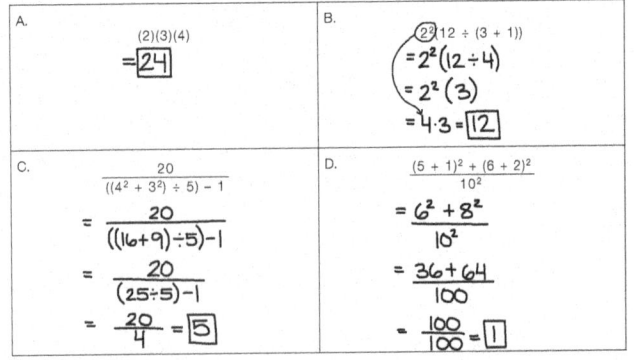

A. $(2)(3)(4) = \boxed{24}$

B. $2^2(12 \div (3+1))$
$= 2^2(12 \div 4)$
$= 2^2(3)$
$= 4 \cdot 3 = \boxed{12}$

C. $\dfrac{20}{((4^2 + 3^2) \div 5) - 1}$
$= \dfrac{20}{((16+9) \div 5) - 1}$
$= \dfrac{20}{(25 \div 5) - 1}$
$= \dfrac{20}{4} = \boxed{5}$

D. $\dfrac{(5+1)^2 + (6+2)^2}{10^2}$
$= \dfrac{6^2 + 8^2}{10^2}$
$= \dfrac{36+64}{100}$
$= \dfrac{100}{100} = \boxed{1}$

Part 2: Simplify each expression using the order of operations. These answers will involve fractions and negative values. **Use parentheses** to show that multiplication and division take precedence over addition and subtraction.

E. $(1 \div 10) + (3 \div 10) + (5 \div 10)$
$= \frac{1}{10} + \frac{3}{10} + \frac{5}{10} = \boxed{\frac{9}{10}}$

F. $(10 \div 1 \times 3 \div 6) - (2 \times 4)$
$= 5 - 8$
$= \boxed{-3}$

G. $6 - (12 \div 6 \times 2) - 10 + 1$
$= 6 - 4 - 10 + 1$
$= 2 - 10 + 1$
$= -8 + 1 = \boxed{-7}$

H. $1 + (2 \times 3 \div 7) + (4 \times 5)$
$= 1 + \frac{6}{7} + 20$
$= \boxed{21\frac{6}{7}}$

I. $3 - (10 \div 5 \times 9 \div 6) - 8$
$= 3 - 3 - 8$
$= \boxed{-8}$

J. $(2 \div 5) + (1 \div 5) + (7 \times 2)$
$= \frac{2}{5} + \frac{1}{5} + 14$
$= \boxed{14\frac{3}{5}}$

Key Points from Demo Video – Lesson 18
Substitution

In Lesson 18, students substitute variables with the values given, then they evaluate each expression.

In Part 1, the substitutions for all four problems are $x = 3$ and $y = 4$. The expressions in Part 1 differ only slightly, so students must pay close attention to these subtle differences (as they have throughout this entire unit):

- $x + y$
- $x - y$
- $-x + y$
- $-x - y$

In Part 2, the substitutions are different for each problem.

Again, all the problems in each row differ only slightly. Boxes, E, F, G, and H show the following expressions:

- $3a + b$
- $3a - b$
- $-3a + b$
- $-3a - b$

Lesson 18: Substitution

Part 1: Substitute, then simplify. $x = 3, y = 4$

A. $x + y = 3 + 4 = \boxed{7}$

B. $x - y = 3 - 4 = \boxed{-1}$

C. $-x + y = -3 + 4 = \boxed{1}$

D. $-x - y = -3 - 4 = \boxed{-7}$

Part 2: Substitute, then simplify. Notice and focus on the subtle differences between the problems in each row.

E. $a = 2, b = 7$
$3a + b = 3(2) + 7 = 6 + 7 = \boxed{13}$

F. $a = 3, b = 8$
$3a - b = 3(3) - 8 = 9 - 8 = \boxed{1}$

G. $a = 5, b = 2$
$-3a + b = -3(5) + 2 = -15 + 2 = \boxed{-13}$

H. $a = 2, b = 3$
$-3a - b = -3(2) - 3 = -6 - 3 = \boxed{-9}$

I. $c = (-10), d = 2$
$c + 4d = -10 + 4(2) = -10 + 8 = \boxed{-2}$

J. $c = 15, d = 1$
$c - 4d = 15 - 4(1) = 15 - 4 = \boxed{11}$

K. $c = 8, d = 2$
$-c + 4d = -(8) + 4(2) = -8 + 8 = \boxed{0}$

L. $c = 3, d = 1$
$-c - 4d = -(3) - 4(1) = -3 - 4 = \boxed{-7}$

M. $e = 2, f = 3$
$3ef + 2e = 3(2)(3) + 2(2) = 18 + 4 = \boxed{22}$

N. $e = 4, f = 2$
$3ef - 2e = 3(4)(2) - 2(4) = 24 - 8 = \boxed{16}$

O. $e = 5, f = 1$
$-3ef + 2e = -3(5)(1) + 2(5) = -15 + 10 = \boxed{-5}$

P. $e = 8, f = 0$
$-3ef - 2e = -3(8)(0) - 2(8) = 0 - 16 = \boxed{-16}$

Q. $g = (-4), h = 5$
$g + gh = (-4) + (-4)(5) = -4 + -20 = \boxed{-24}$

R. $g = (-5), h = (-10)$
$g - gh = (-5) - (-5)(-10) = -5 - 50 = \boxed{-55}$

S. $g = 2, h = 3$
$-g + gh = -(2) + (2)(3) = -2 + 6 = \boxed{4}$

T. $g = 5, h = 3$
$-g - gh = -(5) - (5)(3) = -5 - 15 = \boxed{-20}$

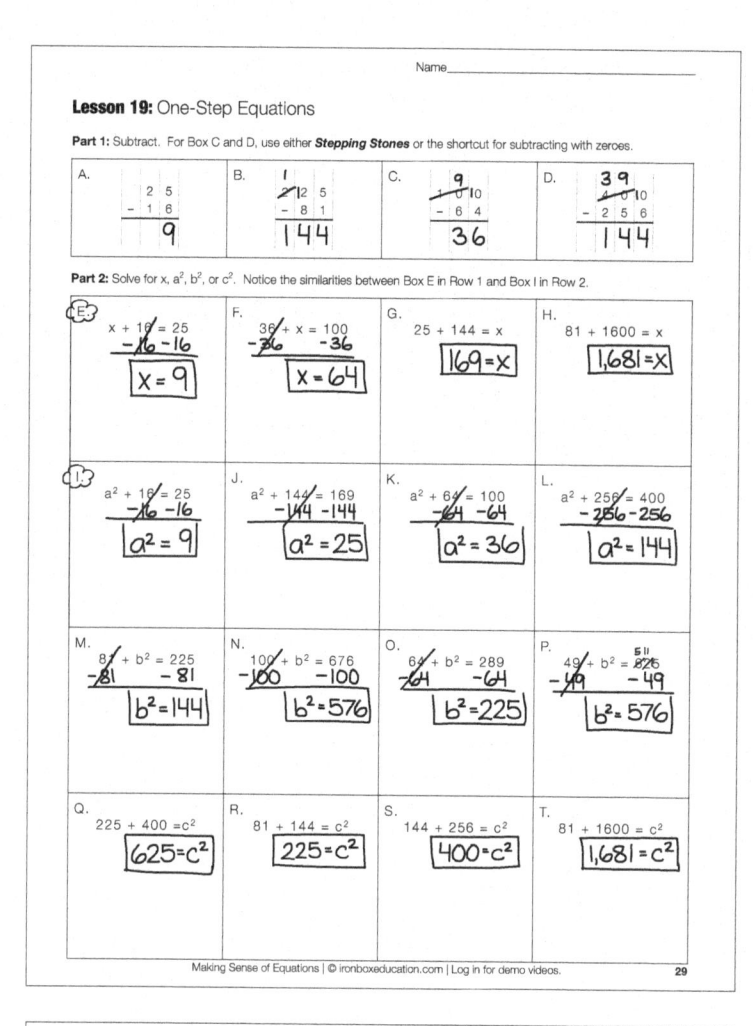

Lesson 19: One-Step Equations

Part 1: Subtract. For Box C and D, use either **Stepping Stones** or the shortcut for subtracting with zeroes.

A. $25 - 16 = 9$	B. $125 - 81 = 144$ (shown as 225 − 81 = 144)	C. $100 - 64 = 36$	D. $310 - 256 = 144$ (400 − 256 = 144)

Part 2: Solve for x, a^2, b^2, or c^2. Notice the similarities between Box E in Row 1 and Box I in Row 2.

E. $x + 16 = 25$; $-16\ -16$; $x = 9$	F. $36 + x = 100$; $-36\ -36$; $x = 64$	G. $25 + 144 = x$; $169 = x$	H. $81 + 1600 = x$; $1,681 = x$
I. $a^2 + 16 = 25$; $-16\ -16$; $a^2 = 9$	J. $a^2 + 144 = 169$; $-144\ -144$; $a^2 = 25$	K. $a^2 + 64 = 100$; $-64\ -64$; $a^2 = 36$	L. $a^2 + 256 = 400$; $-256\ -256$; $a^2 = 144$
M. $81 + b^2 = 225$; $-81\ -81$; $b^2 = 144$	N. $100 + b^2 = 676$; $-100\ -100$; $b^2 = 576$	O. $64 + b^2 = 289$; $-64\ -64$; $b^2 = 225$	P. $49 + b^2 = 625$; $-49\ -49$; $b^2 = 576$
Q. $225 + 400 = c^2$; $625 = c^2$	R. $81 + 144 = c^2$; $225 = c^2$	S. $144 + 256 = c^2$; $400 = c^2$	T. $81 + 1600 = c^2$; $1,681 = c^2$

Lesson 20: Two-Step Equations

Part 1: Evaluate the Squares.

A. $1^2 = 1$	B. $2^2 = 4$	C. $3^2 = 9$	D. $4^2 = 16$	E. $5^2 = 25$
F. $6^2 = 36$	G. $7^2 = 49$	H. $8^2 = 64$	I. $9^2 = 81$	J. $10^2 = 100$

Part 2: Find the square roots (write only the positive root).

K. $\sqrt{9} = 3$	L. $\sqrt{36} = 6$	M. $\sqrt{25} = 5$	N. $\sqrt{81} = 9$	O. $\sqrt{100} = 10$
P. $\sqrt{a^2} = a$	Q. $\sqrt{b^2} = b$	R. $\sqrt{c^2} = c$	S. $\sqrt{x^2} = x$	T. $\sqrt{y^2} = y$

Part 3: Solve for a, b, or c.

Example: $a^2 + 16 = 25$; $-16\ -16$; $\sqrt{a^2} = \sqrt{9}$; $a = 3$	U. $a^2 + 64 = 100$; $-64\ -64$; $\sqrt{a^2} = \sqrt{36}$; $a = 6$	V. $a^2 + 144 = 225$; $-144\ -144$; $\sqrt{a^2} = \sqrt{81}$; $a = 9$	W. $a^2 + 144 = 169$; $-144\ -144$; $\sqrt{a^2} = \sqrt{25}$; $a = 5$
X. $9 + b^2 = 25$; $-9\ -9$; $\sqrt{b^2} = \sqrt{16}$; $b = 4$	Y. $36 + b^2 = 100$; $-36\ -36$; $\sqrt{b^2} = \sqrt{64}$; $b = 8$	Z. $a^2 + 225 = 289$; $-225\ -225$; $\sqrt{a^2} = \sqrt{64}$; $a = 8$	AA. $a^2 + 1600 = 1681$; $-1600\ -1600$; $\sqrt{a^2} = \sqrt{81}$; $a = 9$
AB. $a^2 + 576 = 676$; $-576\ -576$; $\sqrt{a^2} = \sqrt{100}$; $a = 10$	AC. $a^2 + 576 = 625$; $-576\ -576$; $\sqrt{a^2} = \sqrt{49}$; $a = 7$	AD. $9 + 16 = c^2$; $\sqrt{25} = \sqrt{c^2}$; $5 = c$	AE. $36 + 64 = c^2$; $\sqrt{100} = \sqrt{c^2}$; $10 = c$

Key Points from Demo Video – Lesson 19
One-Step Equations

Lesson 19 is a key lesson for the following reasons:

- It reviews one-step equations.
- It lays the foundation for future lessons on the Pythagorean Theorem.

In Part 1, students must subtract accurately using **Stepping Stones** or the shortcut for subtracting with zeroes. These subtraction problems all involve perfect squares, and they will all be used in Part 2.

In Part 2, students use one-step equations to solve for the following:

- Solve for x.
- Solve for a^2.
- Solve for b^2.
- Solve for c^2.

Notice the similarities between Box E and Box I.

- $x + 16 = 25$
- $a^2 + 16 = 25$

Students have not yet learned to find the square root (upcoming lesson), so just solve for a^2, and not for a.

Key Points from Demo Video – Lesson 20
Two-Step Equations

The previous lesson covered one-step equations in preparation for the Pythagorean Theorem.

Lesson 20 takes it to the next level with two step equations.

In Part 1, students evaluate the Squares.

In Part 2, students use the Squares to help them find square roots. Write only the positive root. Boxes P, Q, R, S, and T involve variables instead of numbers.

In Part 3 solve for a or b using two-step equations.

- Step 1: Subtract the correct value from both sides of the equation.
- Step 2: Take the square root of both sides of the equation.

In Box AD and Box AE, solve for c using two-step equations.

- Step 1: Add to make sure both sides of the equation are simplified.
- Step 2: Take the square root of both sides of the equation.

Key Points from Demo Video – Lesson 21
Substitution and Two-Step Equations

In previous lessons, students learned the skill of two-step equations and the separate skill of substitution.

In Lesson 21, these separate skills are combined.

In Part 1, students use substitution. Then, they evaluate exponents.

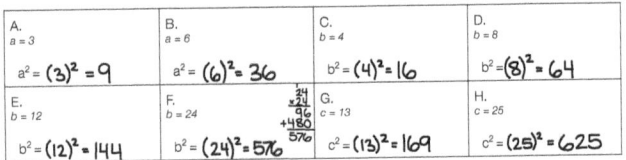

In Part 2, students find square roots (write only the positive root).

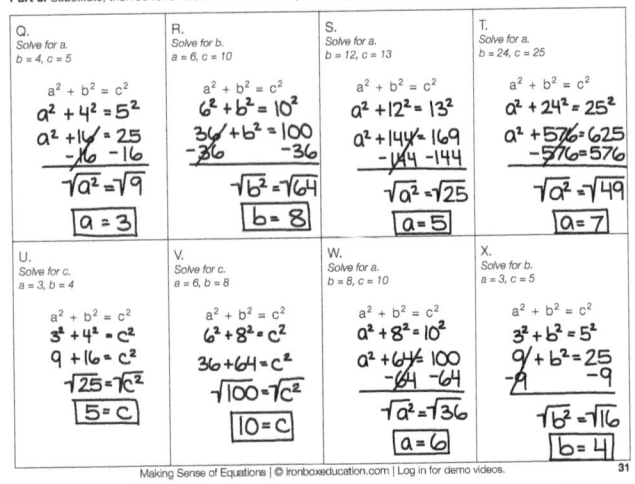

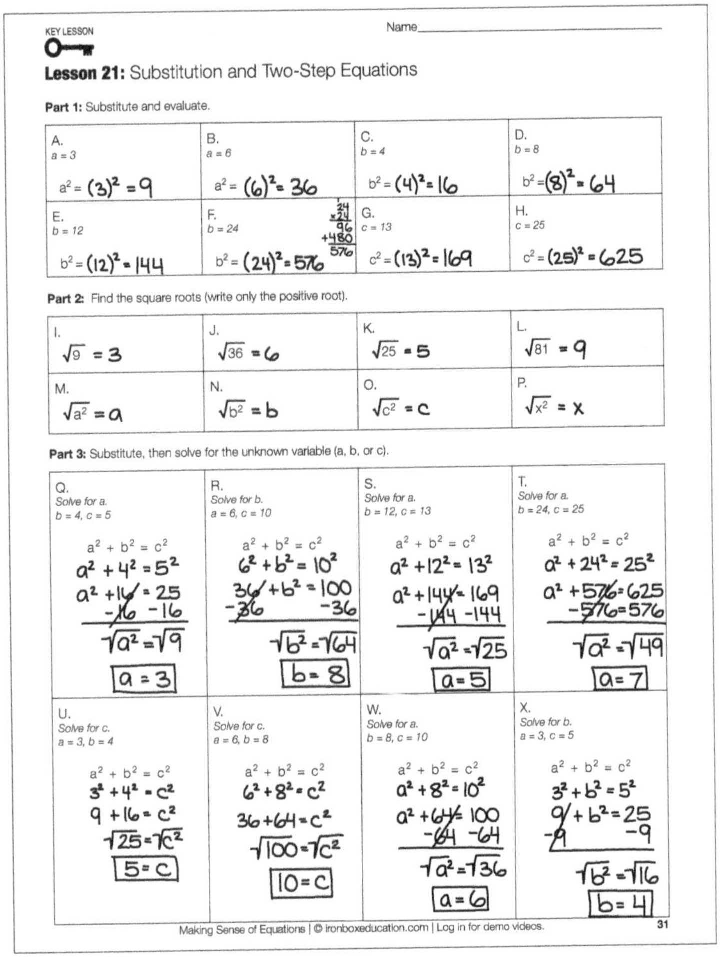

Part 3 includes skills from Part 1 and Part 2. For example, Box Q includes the following steps.

- First, substitute.
- Next, evaluate exponents.
- Finally, solve using a two-step equation.
  - Step 1: Subtract 16 from both sides of the equation.
  - Step 2: Take the square root of both sides of the equation.

As you may have noticed in this lesson, students are using the equation for the Pythagorean Theorem, even though they have not formally learned the Pythagorean Theorem yet.

Key Points from Demo Video – Lesson 22
Measuring Angles

An important geometric equation that students will learn about soon is the Pythagorean Theorem:

- $a^2 + b^2 = c^2$

The Pythagorean Theorem only works for right triangles (triangles with a right angle measuring 90°).

This means that students need to recognize whether or not a a triangle is a right triangle and whether or not the Pythagorean Theorem will work.

Since right angles are so important, Lesson 22 gets students into the mindset of noticing them.

In Part 1, students measure each of the four angles using the protractor. Then, they find the right angle that measures 90° (found in Box D). They corner that 90° angle with a little square, and they label the angle as a "right angle," as shown in the answer key.

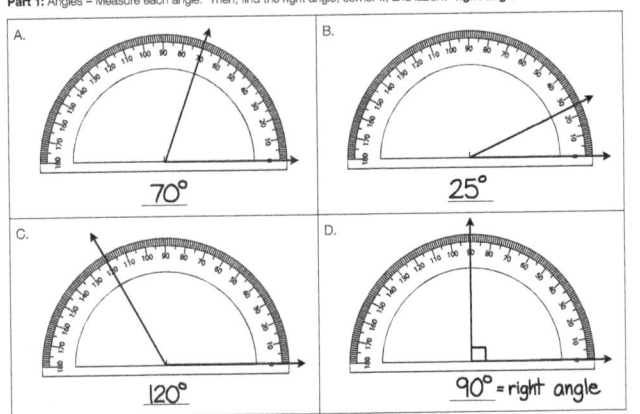

In Part 2, students look for right angles and write "90°" and the words "right angle" next to them. For the other angles, students indicate whether the angles measure < 90° or > 90°.

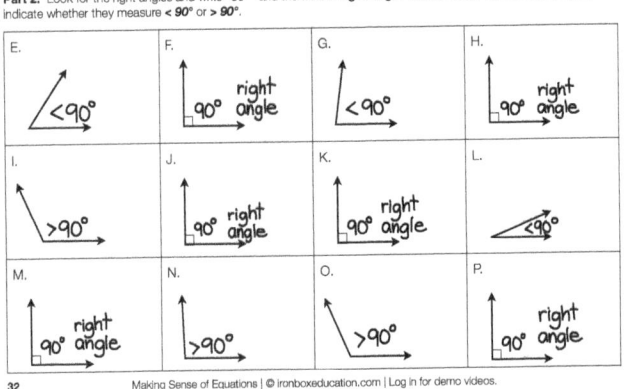

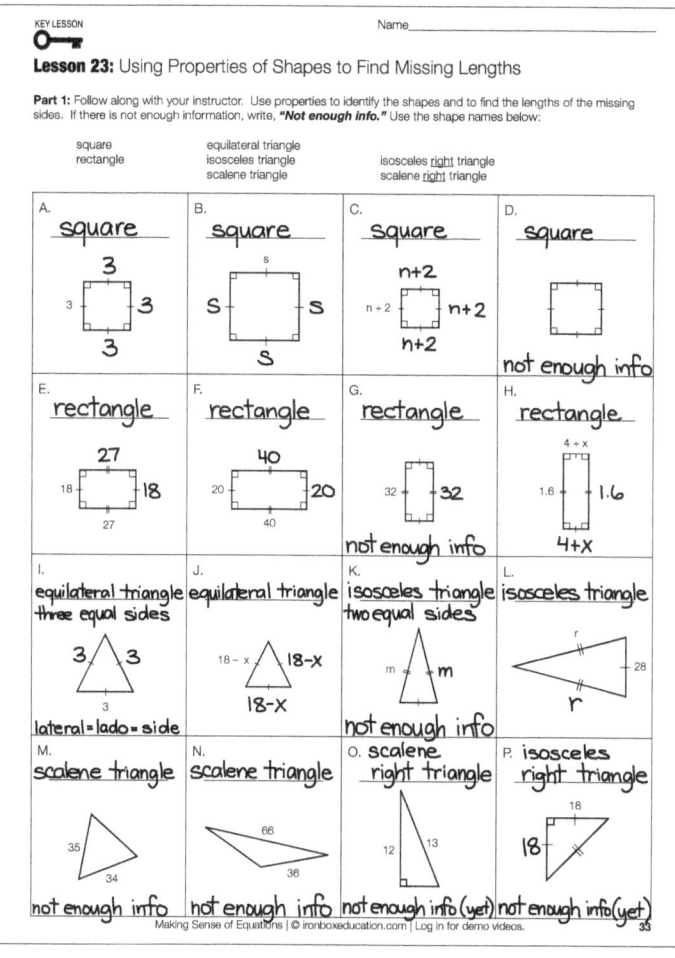

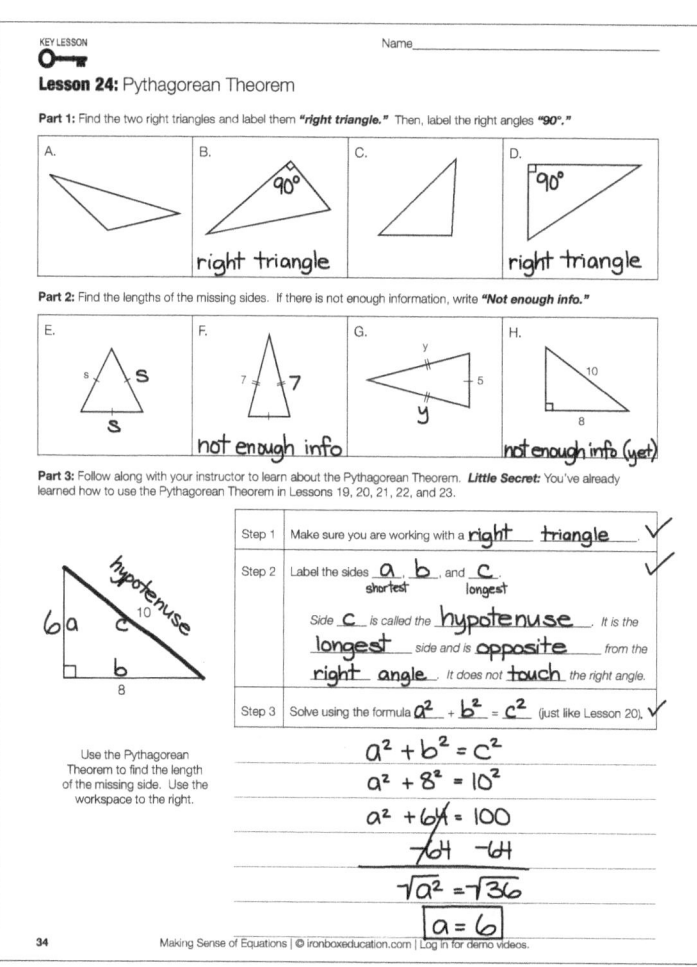

Key Points from Demo Video – Lesson 23
Using Properties of Shapes to Find Missing Lengths

In Lesson 23, students follow along with their instructor to use properties to identify shapes and to find the lengths of the missing sides.

In Box A, for example, a figure with four equal sides and four right angles is a square. Since we know that one side is 3 units long, we know that all four sides of the square are 3 units long.

If there is not enough information to find the length of a missing side, students write, **"Not enough info."**

Five different types of triangles are used:

- equilateral triangle (three equal sides)
- isosceles triangle (two equal sides)
- scalene triangle (no equal sides)
- isosceles right triangle
- scalene right triangle

The previous lesson covered right angles (90°).

In Box O and Box P, students should write, **"Not enough info (yet)."** Students will use the Pythagorean Theorem in the next lesson to find the length of the missing sides of right triangles.

Key Points from Demo Video – Lesson 24
Pythagorean Theorem

The Pythagorean Theorem can be used to find the length of the missing side of a right triangle. Part 1 reviews right triangles.

In Part 2, students find the lengths of the missing sides. There is not enough information in Box F. There is not **yet** enough information in Box H.

In Part 3, students follow along with their instructor to learn how to use the Pythagorean Theorem, as shown in the demo video.

Students apply previously learned skills, including substitution, two-step equations, exponents, and square roots.

Use the following steps:

- Make sure you have a right triangle.
- Label the sides a, b, and c.
  - Side a is the shortest.
  - Side c is the longest. It is called the hypotenuse. It is opposite from the right angle, and it does not touch the right angle.
- Solve using the formula $a^2 + b^2 = c^2$.

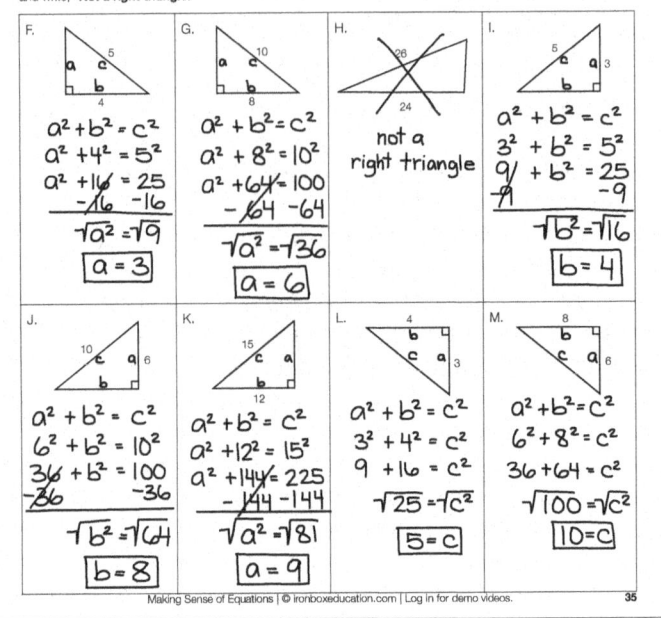

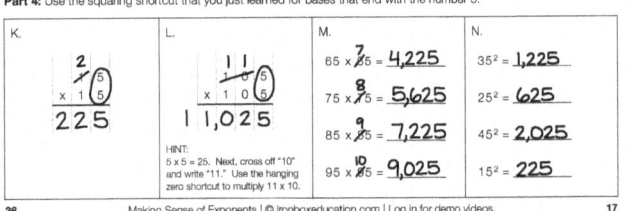

Key Points from Demo Video – Lesson 25
Pythagorean Theorem

In the previous lesson, students learned how to use the Pythagorean Theorem to find the length of a missing side of a right triangle.

In Lesson 25, students practice using the Pythagorean Theorem.

Part 1 provides a review of squaring numbers and subtracting numbers. In Box C and Box D, either use **Stepping Stones** or the shortcut for subtracting with zeroes. Every problem in Part 1 will reappear in Part 2.

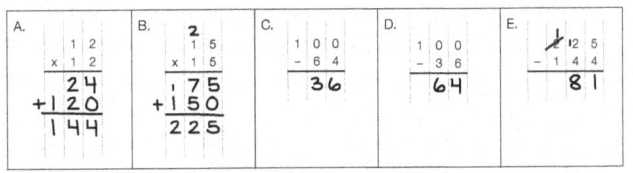

In Part 2, students solve using the Pythagorean Theorem. Label the sides a, b, and c first. Side a is the shortest side, and side c is the longest side (hypotenuse).

Be careful since the right angle changes positions from problem to problem.

One of the triangles is not a right triangle (Box H). Students should cross it out and write, **"Not a right triangle."** This problem is included to help students remember that the Pythagorean Theorem only works with right triangles.

Key Points from Demo Video – Lesson 26
Squaring Shortcut #1

Since the Pythagorean Theorem involves squaring numbers, it's helpful to students if they can quickly find the square of a number.

Lesson 26 introduces the **very elegant Squaring Shortcut #1.**

This shortcut only works when squaring bases that end with 5 (i.e., 25^2, 35^2, 45^2, and so on).

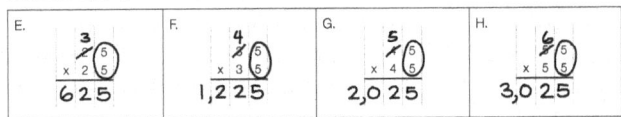

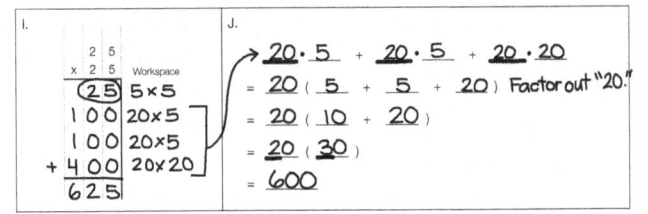

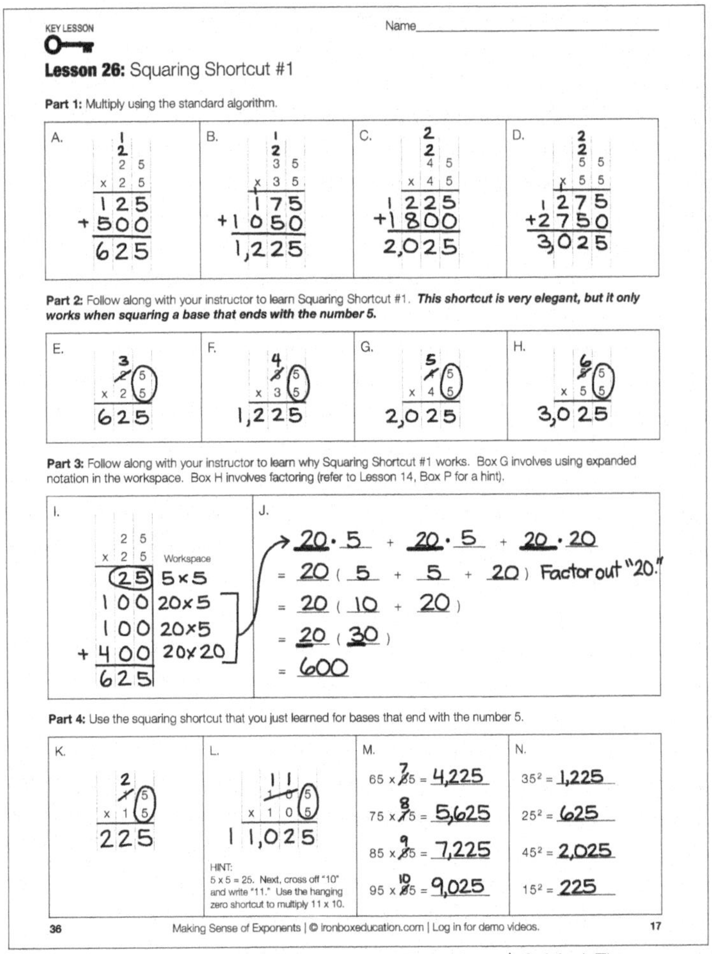

In Part 1, students multiply the long way using the standard algorithm.

In Part 2, students follow along with their instructor to multiply the exact same numbers using the squaring shortcut, as shown in the demo video. In Box E:

- Circle the 5's in the ones place values. 5 x 5 is 25, so write down 25.
- Cross off the 2 in the number on top and count up by one, which gives you 3. 2 x 3 is 6, so write it down. The answer is 625.

As shown in the demo video, Part 3 explains why Squaring Shortcut #1 works.

Lesson 27: Squaring Shortcut #2; Memorizing 11^2 Through 15^2

The next lesson (Lesson 28) will be much easier if you can memorize the following: 11^2, 12^2, 13^2, 14^2, and 15^2.

Since the number 15 ends with a "5," you can easily figure out 15^2 by using the very elegant Squaring Shortcut #1. The numbers 11, 12, 13, and 14 do not end with a "5," so you can't use Squaring Shortcut #1. However, there is a different shortcut that you can use to help you memorize their squares (although <u>it's not nearly as elegant</u>).

Use this shortcut only for squaring two-digit numbers that begin with "1" (the numbers 11-19).

Part 1: Follow along with your instructor to complete this lesson.

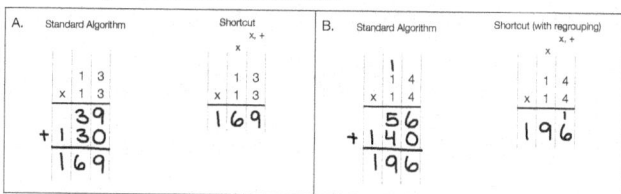

A. Standard Algorithm: $13 \times 13 = 39 + 130 = 169$ Shortcut: 169
B. Standard Algorithm: $14 \times 14 = 56 + 140 = 196$ Shortcut (with regrouping): 196

Part 2: Use the squaring shortcut.

C. $12 \times 12 = 144$
D. $11 \times 11 = 121$
E. $19 \times 19 = 361$
F. $17 \times 17 = 289$

Part 3: Work on one column at a time to <u>memorize</u> the squares shown below.

- First, study the problems in each box in your mind, and make sure you can recall the answers instantly. Here are a couple of tips: 15^2 has been previously learned using the elegant Squaring Shortcut #1. Also, notice how you can memorize 13^2 and 14^2 together since their products (169 and 196) look similar to each other.
- Next, write down your answers.
- Then, move on to the next column and repeat the two steps above. Cover up your previous answers when you move on to the next column.

G.
$11^2 = 121$
$12^2 = 144$
$13^2 = 169$
$14^2 = 196$
$15^2 = 225$

H.
$12^2 = 144$
$11^2 = 121$
$15^2 = 225$
$13^2 = 169$
$14^2 = 196$

I.
$13^2 = 169$
$15^2 = 225$
$12^2 = 144$
$11^2 = 121$
$14^2 = 196$

J.
$14^2 = 196$
$13^2 = 169$
$11^2 = 121$
$15^2 = 225$
$12^2 = 144$

K.
$15^2 = 225$
$14^2 = 196$
$13^2 = 169$
$12^2 = 144$
$11^2 = 121$

Lesson 28: Pythagorean Theorem

Part 1: Write the answers to the following squares, which you memorized from the previous lesson.

A. $11^2 = 121$
B. $12^2 = 144$
C. $13^2 = 169$
D. $14^2 = 196$
E. $15^2 = 225$

Part 2: Find the square roots.

F. $\sqrt{196} = 14$
G. $\sqrt{169} = 13$
H. $\sqrt{225} = 15$
I. $\sqrt{121} = 11$
J. $\sqrt{144} = 12$

Part 3: Use the Pythagorean Theorem ($a^2 + b^2 = c^2$) to find the length of the missing side. Label sides a, b, and c first (a = shortest, c = longest). Be careful since the right angle changes positions from problem to problem.

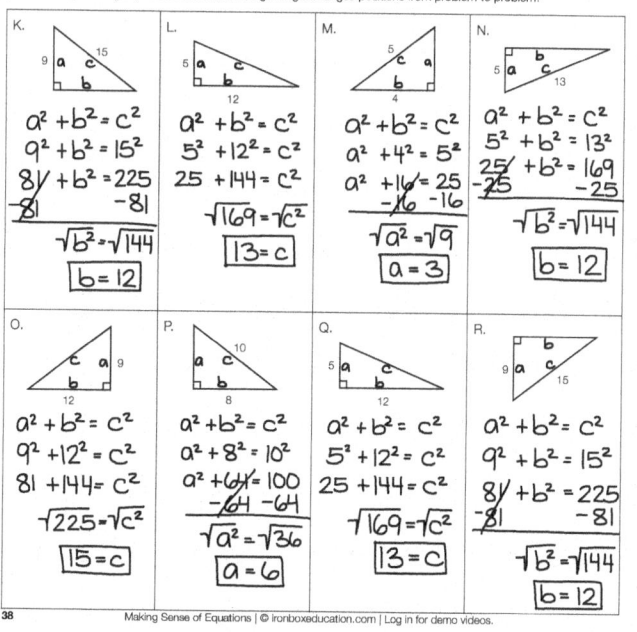

K. (9, b, 15)
$a^2 + b^2 = c^2$
$9^2 + b^2 = 15^2$
$81 + b^2 = 225$
$-81 \quad -81$
$\sqrt{b^2} = \sqrt{144}$
$b = 12$

L. (5, 12, c)
$a^2 + b^2 = c^2$
$5^2 + 12^2 = c^2$
$25 + 144 = c^2$
$\sqrt{169} = \sqrt{c^2}$
$13 = c$

M. (a, 4, 5)
$a^2 + b^2 = c^2$
$a^2 + 4^2 = 5^2$
$a^2 + 16 = 25$
$-16 \quad -16$
$\sqrt{a^2} = \sqrt{9}$
$a = 3$

N. (5, b, 13)
$a^2 + b^2 = c^2$
$5^2 + b^2 = 13^2$
$25 + b^2 = 169$
$-25 \quad -25$
$\sqrt{b^2} = \sqrt{144}$
$b = 12$

O. (c, 9, 12)
$a^2 + b^2 = c^2$
$9^2 + 12^2 = c^2$
$81 + 144 = c^2$
$\sqrt{225} = \sqrt{c^2}$
$15 = c$

P. (10, a, 8)
$a^2 + b^2 = c^2$
$a^2 + 8^2 = 10^2$
$a^2 + 64 = 100$
$-64 \quad -64$
$\sqrt{a^2} = \sqrt{36}$
$a = 6$

Q. (5, 12, c)
$a^2 + b^2 = c^2$
$5^2 + 12^2 = c^2$
$25 + 144 = c^2$
$\sqrt{169} = \sqrt{c^2}$
$13 = c$

R. (9, b, 15)
$a^2 + b^2 = c^2$
$9^2 + b^2 = 15^2$
$81 + b^2 = 225$
$-81 \quad -81$
$\sqrt{b^2} = \sqrt{144}$
$b = 12$

Key Points from Demo Video – Lesson 27
Squaring Shortcut #2; Memorizing 11^2 Through 15^2

The next lesson (Lesson 28) will be much easier if students can memorize 11^2, 12^2, 13^2, 14^2, and 15^2. Lesson 27 helps students memorize these facts.

Since the number 15 ends with a "5," you can easily figure out 15^2 by using the very elegant Squaring Shortcut #1.

The numbers 11, 12, 13, and 14 do not end with a "5," so you can't use Squaring Shortcut #1. However, there is another squaring shortcut that students can use to help them memorize these squares, *although it's not nearly as elegant.* Use this shortcut only for squaring two-digit numbers that begin with "1" (the numbers 11-19).

As shown in the demo video, the steps are:

- Ones place value – multiply, then add.
- Tens place value – multiply.

Some of the problems require regrouping, so be sure to watch the demo video carefully. Since this shortcut is not as elegant, students should memorize 11^2, 12^2, 13^2, 14^2, and 15^2 instead. *Part 3 gives tips to help students memorize these facts.*

Key Points from Demo Video – Lesson 28
Pythagorean Theorem

In Lesson 28, students continue practicing the Pythagorean Theorem. These problems include more difficult squares, including 12^2, 13^2, and 15^2. Students memorized these facts in the previous lesson.

In Part 1, students review 11^2, 12^2, 13^2, 14^2, and 15^2.

In Part 2, students find the square roots of 121, 144, 169, 196, and 225.

Some of the problems in Part 1 and Part 2 will reappear in Part 3.

Students should be careful because the right angle changes position from problem to problem. This means that the locations of sides a, b, and c may change from problem to problem as well.

Students need to accurately identify side c (the hypotenuse) in order for the Pythagorean Theorem to work.

Lesson 29: Approximating Square Roots

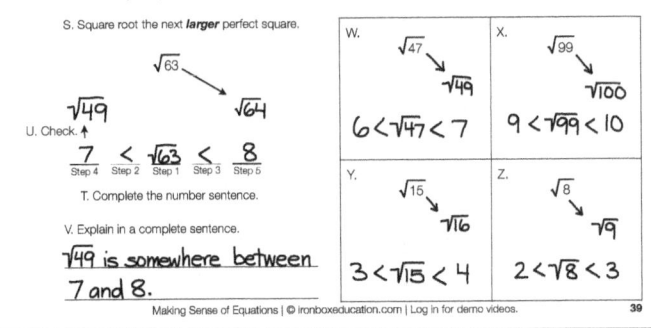

Part 1: Find the square roots of perfect squares.

A. $\sqrt{25}$ = 5	B. $\sqrt{4}$ = 2	C. $\sqrt{36}$ = 6	D. $\sqrt{64}$ = 8	E. $\sqrt{100}$ = 10
F. $\sqrt{16}$ = 4	G. $\sqrt{1}$ = 1	H. $\sqrt{49}$ = 7	I. $\sqrt{81}$ = 9	J. $\sqrt{9}$ = 3

Part 2: Follow along with your instructor to approximate square roots of non-perfect squares by approximating **down**.

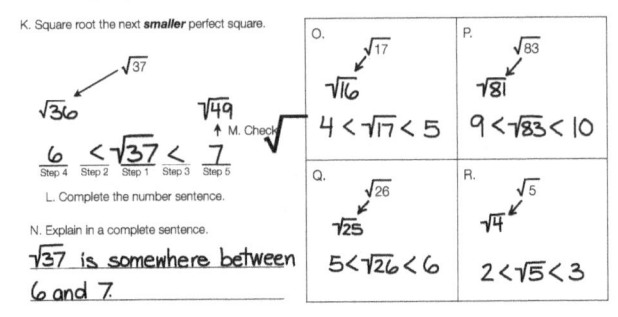

K. Square root the next *smaller* perfect square.

$\sqrt{37}$
$\sqrt{36}$ $\sqrt{49}$ M. Check
6 < $\sqrt{37}$ < 7
Step 4, Step 2, Step 1, Step 3, Step 5

L. Complete the number sentence.

N. Explain in a complete sentence.
$\sqrt{37}$ is somewhere between 6 and 7.

O. $\sqrt{17}$, $\sqrt{16}$: 4 < $\sqrt{17}$ < 5	P. $\sqrt{83}$, $\sqrt{81}$: 9 < $\sqrt{83}$ < 10
Q. $\sqrt{26}$, $\sqrt{25}$: 5 < $\sqrt{26}$ < 6	R. $\sqrt{5}$, $\sqrt{4}$: 2 < $\sqrt{5}$ < 3

Part 3: Follow along with your instructor to approximate square roots of non-perfect squares by approximating **up**.

S. Square root the next *larger* perfect square.

$\sqrt{63}$
$\sqrt{49}$ $\sqrt{64}$
U. Check: 7 < $\sqrt{63}$ < 8
Step 4, Step 2, Step 1, Step 3, Step 5

T. Complete the number sentence.

V. Explain in a complete sentence.
$\sqrt{49}$ is somewhere between 7 and 8.

W. $\sqrt{47}$, $\sqrt{49}$: 6 < $\sqrt{47}$ < 7	X. $\sqrt{99}$, $\sqrt{100}$: 9 < $\sqrt{99}$ < 10
Y. $\sqrt{15}$, $\sqrt{16}$: 3 < $\sqrt{15}$ < 4	Z. $\sqrt{8}$, $\sqrt{9}$: 2 < $\sqrt{8}$ < 3

Lesson 30: Approximating Square Roots

Part 1: Find the square roots of perfect squares.

A. $\sqrt{49}$ = 7	B. $\sqrt{1}$ = 1	C. $\sqrt{81}$ = 9	D. $\sqrt{9}$ = 3	E. $\sqrt{16}$ = 4
F. $\sqrt{100}$ = 10	G. $\sqrt{4}$ = 2	H. $\sqrt{25}$ = 5	I. $\sqrt{36}$ = 6	J. $\sqrt{64}$ = 8

Part 2: Follow along with your instructor to approximate square roots of non-perfect squares by approximating **up or down**. Before solving, decide whether you will approximate up or down by drawing the appropriate arrows. Indicate which integer your answer is closer to (i.e., the square root of 17 is between 4 and 5, but is closer to 4).

Example: $\sqrt{17}$, $\sqrt{16}$: 4 < $\sqrt{17}$ < 5, closer to 4	K. $\sqrt{80}$, $\sqrt{81}$: 8 < $\sqrt{80}$ < 9, closer to 9	L. $\sqrt{60}$, $\sqrt{64}$: 7 < $\sqrt{60}$ < 8, closer to 8	M. $\sqrt{37}$, $\sqrt{36}$: 6 < $\sqrt{37}$ < 7, closer to 6
N. $\sqrt{3}$, $\sqrt{4}$: 1 < $\sqrt{3}$ < 2, closer to 2	O. $\sqrt{15}$, $\sqrt{16}$: 3 < $\sqrt{15}$ < 4, closer to 4	P. $\sqrt{50}$, $\sqrt{49}$: 7 < $\sqrt{50}$ < 8, closer to 7	Q. $\sqrt{103}$, $\sqrt{100}$: 10 < $\sqrt{103}$ < 11, closer to 10
R. $\sqrt{23}$, $\sqrt{25}$: 4 < $\sqrt{23}$ < 5, closer to 5	S. $\sqrt{39}$, $\sqrt{36}$: 6 < $\sqrt{39}$ < 7, closer to 6	T. $\sqrt{20}$, $\sqrt{16}$: 4 < $\sqrt{20}$ < 5, closer to 4	U. $\sqrt{18}$, $\sqrt{16}$: 4 < $\sqrt{18}$ < 5, closer to 4
V. $\sqrt{7}$, $\sqrt{9}$: 2 < $\sqrt{7}$ < 3, closer to 3	W. $\sqrt{2}$, $\sqrt{1}$: 1 < $\sqrt{2}$ < 2, closer to 1	X. $\sqrt{95}$, $\sqrt{100}$: 9 < $\sqrt{95}$ < 10, closer to 10	Y. $\sqrt{85}$, $\sqrt{81}$: 9 < $\sqrt{85}$ < 10, closer to 9

Key Points from Demo Video – Lesson 29
Approximating Square Roots

So far, students have been working with square roots of perfect squares, which are easy to solve. For example:

$$\sqrt{36} = 6 \text{ (since } 6 \times 6 = 36\text{)}$$

$$\sqrt{64} = 8 \text{ (since } 8 \times 8 = 64\text{)}$$

Lesson 29 focuses on square roots of numbers that are not perfect squares, such as 37 and 63.

In Part 2, students follow along with their instructor to approximate square roots of non-perfect squares by **approximating down.** The number 37 is not a perfect square, but the closest perfect square is 36 (found by approximating down).

The demo video shows how to help students see that the square root of 37 is somewhere between 6 and 7.

$$6 < \sqrt{37} < 7$$

In Part 3, students approximate square roots of non-perfect squares by **approximating up.**

Key Points from Demo Video – Lesson 30
Approximating Square Roots

In Lesson 29, students approximated the square roots of non-perfect squares by **approximating up.** Then, they approximated the square roots of non-perfect squares by **approximating down.**

Lesson 30 takes it to the next level. Students must:

- decide whether to approximate up **or** down
- indicate which whole number the approximate square root is closer to

Part 1 reviews the square roots of perfect squares, which will be helpful in Part 2.

In Part 2, students follow along with their instructor to learn whether they should approximate up or down. The example uses $\sqrt{17}$. The number 17 is closest to the perfect square of 16, so students approximate down to 16, and $\sqrt{16}$ is 4. Using the procedure from the previous lesson:

$$4 < \sqrt{17} < 5$$

The square root of 17 is somewhere between 4 and 5, but is closer to 4.

Lesson 31: Absolute Value

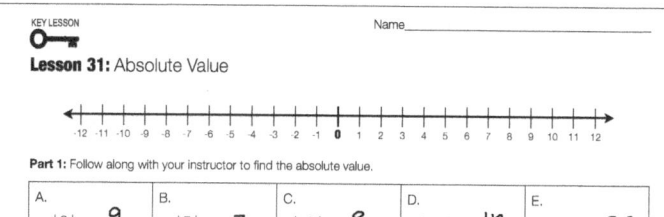

Part 1: Follow along with your instructor to find the absolute value.

A. |9| = 9 |-9| = 9	B. |7| = 7 |-7| = 7	C. |-8| = 8 |8| = 8	D. |42| = 42 |-42| = 42	E. |3.2| = 3.2 |-3.2| = 3.2

Part 2: Follow along with your instructor to compare parentheses versus absolute value symbols.

F. (-4 - 5) = -9 vs. |-4 - 5| = |-9| = 9	G. (6 - -7) = 13 vs. |6 - -7| = |13| = 13	H. (-8 + 3) = -5 vs. |-8 + 3| = |-5| = 5	I. (-4 + 2) = -2 vs. |-4 + 2| = |-2| = 2

Part 3: Evaluate each expression.

J. (-5 + +2) = -3	K. (-5 + -2) = -7	L. (-5 - +2) = -7	M. (-5 - -2) = -3
N. (5 + +2) = 7	O. (5 + -2) = 3	P. (5 - +2) = 3	Q. (5 - -2) = 7

Part 4: Evaluate each expression.

R. |-5 + -2| = |-7| = 7	S. |-5 + +2| = |-3| = 3	T. |-5 - +2| = |-3| = 3	U. |-5 - -2| = |-7| = 7
V. |5 + -2| = |3| = 3	W. |5 + +2| = |7| = 7	X. |5 - +2| = |7| = 7	Y. |5 - -2| = |3| = 3

Key Points from Demo Video – Lesson 31
Absolute Value

When students learned about the order of operations, they learned about parentheses as **grouping symbols.**

Another set of important grouping symbols that are related to parentheses are absolute value symbols.

The absolute value of a number is it's distance from zero.

- The absolute value just tells you <u>how far</u> a number is from zero.
- However, it is **not** interested in <u>which direction</u> a number is from zero.

This explains why absolute values are always positive and never negative (the negative sign tells us to switch directions on the number line).

If you have a negative number in the absolute value symbols, just omit the negative sign.

If there is an expression inside the absolute value symbols, evaluate the expression first as you normally would, then take the absolute value.

Lesson 32: Absolute Value

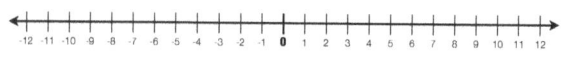

Part 1: Follow along with your instructor to find the absolute value.

A. |5| = 5 |-5| = 5	B. |3| = 3 |-3| = 3	C. |-4| = 4 |4| = 4	D. |85| = 85 |-85| = 85	E. |1.3| = 1.3 |-1.3| = 1.3

Part 2: Evaluate each expression.

Example | -2 - 6 | + | -7 + 3 | = 8 + 4 = 12	F. | 2 + 6 | + | 7 + 3 | = 8 + 10 = 18	G. | 2 - 6 | - | -7 + 3 | = 4 - 4 = 0
H. | -2 - 6 | - | 7 + 3 | = 8 - 10 = -2	I. | 2 - 6 | + | 7 + 3 | = 4 + 4 = 8	J. | 2 - 6 | + | 7 + 3 | = 4 + 10 = 14
K. | -2 + 6 | + | -7 + 3 | = 4 + 4 = 8	L. | 2 + 6 | - | -7 - 3 | = 8 - 10 = -2	M. | 2 + 6 | - | 7 - 3 | = 8 - 4 = 4
N. | -2 + 6 | - | -7 + 3 | = 4 - 10 = -6	O. | 2 + 6 | - | -7 - 3 | = 4 - 10 = -6	P. | -2 + 6 | - | -7 - 3 | = 4 - 4 = 0

Key Points from Demo Video – Lesson 32
Absolute Value

In Lesson 31, students learned about finding the absolute value.

In Lesson 32, students evaluate absolute value expressions such as:

$$| -2 - 6 | - | 7 + 3 |$$

Remember that absolute value symbols are grouping symbols, just like parentheses.

Evaluate the expressions inside each set of absolute value symbols, then take the absolute value.

Be careful with Boxes H, L, N, and O. In these problems a larger absolute value is being subtracted from a smaller absolute value, so the result will be **negative.** Here is a closer look at Box H.

$$| -2 - 6 | - | 7 + 3 |$$
$$= 8 - 10$$
$$= \boxed{-2}$$

Lesson 33: Geometric Equations

Part 1: Simplify. Notice the similarities between the first row of problems and the second row of problems.

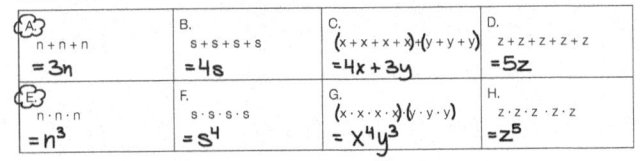

A. $n+n+n$ $= 3n$	B. $s+s+s+s$ $= 4s$	C. $(x+x+x+x)+(y+y+y)$ $= 4x+3y$	D. $z+z+z+z+z$ $= 5z$
E. $n \cdot n \cdot n$ $= n^3$	F. $s \cdot s \cdot s \cdot s$ $= s^4$	G. $(x \cdot x \cdot x \cdot x)(y \cdot y \cdot y)$ $= x^4 y^3$	H. $z \cdot z \cdot z \cdot z \cdot z$ $= z^5$

Part 2: Factor.

I. $5d + 25e$ $= 5(d+5e)$	J. $2d + 2e$ $= 2(d+e)$	K. $12f + 16g$ $= 4(3f+4g)$	L. $2f + 2g$ $= 2(f+g)$

Part 3: Solve. For the last row, take care of the **numbers** first, then take care of the **units**.

M. Solve for P. $s=3$ $P = 4s$ $= 4(3)$ $= \boxed{12}$	N. Solve for P. $s=8$ $P=4s$ $=4(8)$ $=\boxed{32}$	O. Solve for P. $\ell=3, w=5$ $P=2(\ell+w)$ $=2(3+5)$ $=2(8)$ $=\boxed{16}$	P. Solve for P. $\ell=4, w=6$ $P=2(\ell+w)$ $=2(4+6)$ $=2(10)$ $=\boxed{20}$
Q. Solve for A. $s=3$ $A=s^2$ $=(3)^2$ $=\boxed{9}$	R. Solve for A. $s=8$ $A=s^2$ $=(8)^2$ $=\boxed{64}$	S. Solve for A. $\ell=3, w=5$ $A=\ell \cdot w$ $=3 \cdot 5$ $=\boxed{15}$	T. Solve for A. $\ell=4, w=6$ $A=\ell \cdot w$ $=4 \cdot 6$ $=\boxed{24}$
U. Solve for P. $s=3$ in. $P=4s$ $=4(3\text{in})$ $=\boxed{12\text{ in}}$	V. Solve for P. $\ell=3\text{ in}, w=5\text{ in}$ $P=2(\ell+w)$ $=2(3\text{in}+5\text{in})$ $=2(8\text{in})$ $=\boxed{16\text{ in}}$	W. Solve for A. $s=3$ in. $A=s^2$ $=(3\text{in})^2$ $=(3\text{in})(3\text{in})$ $=\boxed{9\text{ in}^2}$	X. Solve for A. $\ell=3\text{ in}, w=5\text{ in}$ $A=\ell \cdot w$ $=(3\text{in})(5\text{in})$ $=\boxed{15\text{ in}^2}$

Lesson 34: Difference Between Perimeter and Area of Squares and Rectangles

Part 1: Follow along with your instructor to compare the perimeter and area of a **square**.

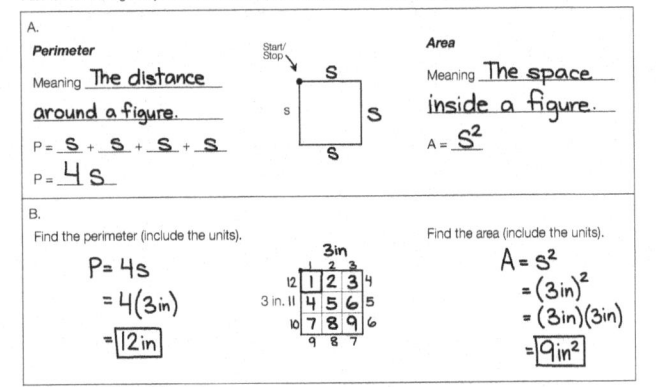

A.
Perimeter — Meaning: The distance around a figure.
$P = s + s + s + s$
$P = 4s$

Area — Meaning: The space inside a figure.
$A = s^2$

B. Find the perimeter (include the units).
$P = 4s$
$= 4(3\text{in})$
$= \boxed{12\text{in}}$

Find the area (include the units).
$A = s^2$
$= (3\text{in})^2$
$= (3\text{in})(3\text{in})$
$= \boxed{9\text{in}^2}$

Part 2: Follow along with your instructor to compare the perimeter and area of a **rectangle**.

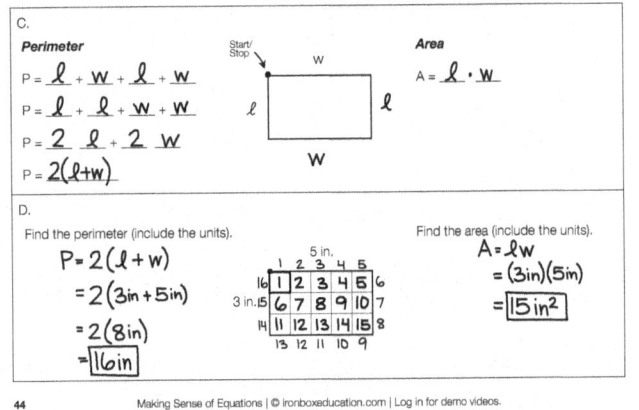

C.
Perimeter
$P = \ell + w + \ell + w$
$P = \ell + \ell + w + w$
$P = 2\ell + 2w$
$P = 2(\ell+w)$

Area
$A = \ell \cdot w$

D. Find the perimeter (include the units).
$P = 2(\ell+w)$
$= 2(3\text{in}+5\text{in})$
$= 2(8\text{in})$
$= \boxed{16\text{in}}$

Find the area (include the units).
$A = \ell w$
$= (3\text{in})(5\text{in})$
$= \boxed{15\text{in}^2}$

Key Points from Demo Video – Lesson 33
Geometric Equations

In Lesson 33, students begin working with geometric equations.

In Part 1, students simplify expressions. Notice the similarities between the first row of problems and the second row of problems. For instance, here are the expressions from Box A and Box E.

- $n + n + n$
- $n \cdot n \cdot n$

In Part 2, students factor expressions, as they did in Lesson 14.

In Part 3, students substitute values into each equation, then they solve each equation.

- Problems M-T (first two rows) involve substituting <u>numbers</u> for each variable.
- Problems U-X (last row) involve substituting <u>numbers and units</u> for each variable.

Operations that are applied to <u>numbers</u> must also be applied to <u>units</u>. Box W shows that one of the steps is $(3\text{ in})^2$. Both the "3" and the "inches" need to be squared, giving you 9 in^2 (and not just 9 in).

Key Points from Demo Video – Lesson 34
Difference Between Perimeter and Area of Squares and Rectangles

In Part 1, students follow along with their instructor to derive the formula for the perimeter and the area of a square.

- The perimeter measures the <u>distance around</u> the square. Here, it is measured in <u>inches</u> (in).
- The area measures the <u>space inside</u> the square. Here, it is measured in <u>square inches</u> (in^2), as shown in the demo video.

In Part 2, students follow along with their instructor to derive the formula for the perimeter and the area of a rectangle.

- The perimeter measures the <u>distance around</u> the rectangle. Here, it is measured in <u>inches</u> (in).
- The area measures the <u>space inside</u> the rectangle. Here, it is measured in <u>square inches</u> (in^2).

During this lesson, students apply skills that they practiced in the previous lesson (Lesson 33), including simplifying, factoring, and substituting.

Lesson 35: Perimeter and Area of Squares and Rectangles

Part 1: Find the perimeter and area of each *square*.

A.
Find the perimeter (include the units).

$P = 4s$
$= 4(5\text{mi})$
$= \boxed{20\text{mi}}$

[square with sides 5 mi]

Find the area (include the units).

$A = s^2$
$= (5\text{mi})^2$
$= \boxed{25\text{mi}^2}$

B.
Find the perimeter (include the units).

$P = 4s$
$= 4(15\text{cm})$
$= \boxed{60\text{cm}}$

[square with sides 15 cm]

Find the area (include the units).

$A = s^2$
$= (15\text{cm})^2$
$= \boxed{225\text{cm}^2}$

Part 2: Find the perimeter and area of each *rectangle*.

C.
Find the perimeter (include the units).

$P = 2(\ell+w)$
$= 2(10\text{in} + 5\text{in})$
$= 2(15\text{in})$
$= \boxed{30\text{in}}$

[rectangle 10 in by 5 in]

Find the area (include the units).

$A = \ell \cdot w$
$= (10\text{in})(5\text{in})$
$= \boxed{50\text{in}^2}$

D.
Find the perimeter (include the units).

$P = 2(\ell+w)$
$= 2(2\text{yd} + 8\text{yd})$
$= 2(10\text{yd})$
$= \boxed{20\text{yd}}$

[rectangle 8 yd by 2 yd]

Find the area (include the units).

$A = \ell w$
$= (2\text{yd})(8\text{yd})$
$= \boxed{16\text{yd}^2}$

KEY LESSON

Lesson 36: Geometric Word Problems

Part 1: Follow along with your instructor to answer the questions about the rectangular pool below. **All four corners of the pool are right angles and measure 90°.** Include the correct units (ft or ft²) in all your answers.

A. Find the perimeter of the pool.

$P = 2(\ell+w)$
$= 2(40\text{ft} + 30\text{ft})$
$= 2(70\text{ft})$
$= \boxed{140\text{ft}}$

B. Find the area of the pool.

$A = \ell \cdot w$
$= (40\text{ft})(30\text{ft})$
$= \boxed{1{,}200\text{ft}^2}$

C. A swimmer swims the length of the pool (40 ft) eight times. What was the total distance that she swam?

$d = \text{distance}$
$d = 8\ell$
$= 8(40\text{ft})$
$= \boxed{320\text{ft}}$

D. A swimmer swims diagonally across the pool from one corner to the opposite corner, as shown in the diagram. How far did she swim?

$a^2 + b^2 = c^2$
$(30\text{ft})^2 + (40\text{ft})^2 = c^2$
$900\text{ft}^2 + 1600\text{ft}^2 = c^2$
$\sqrt{2500\text{ft}^2} = \sqrt{c^2}$
$\boxed{50\text{ft} = c}$

[Diagram of rectangular pool with sides a = 30 ft, b = 40 ft, diagonal c. All four corners of the pool are right angles and measure 90°.]

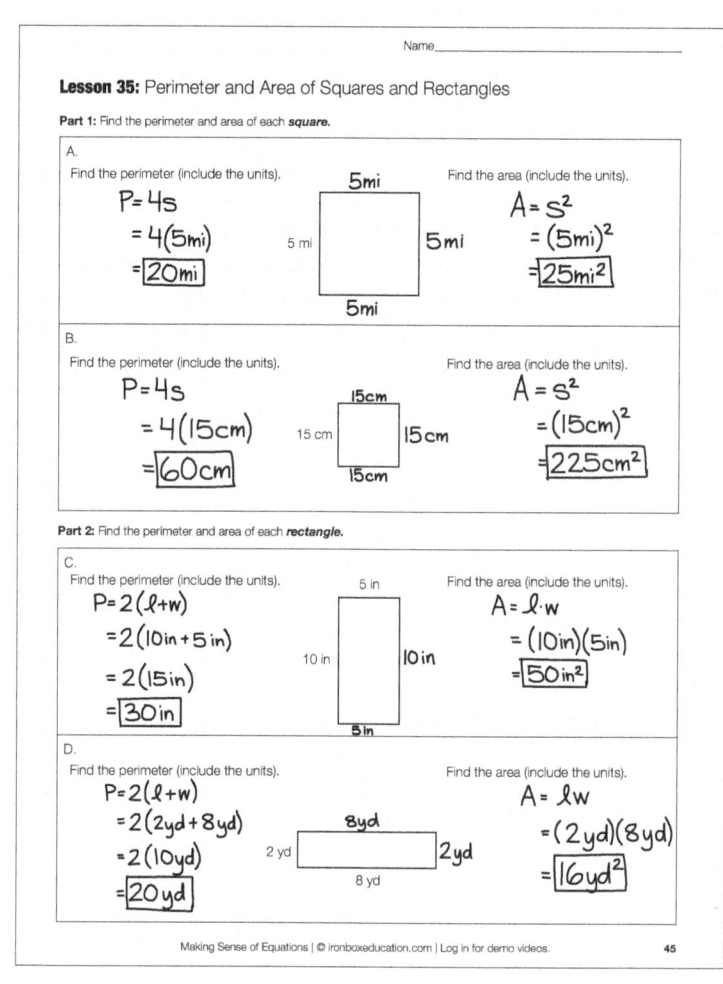

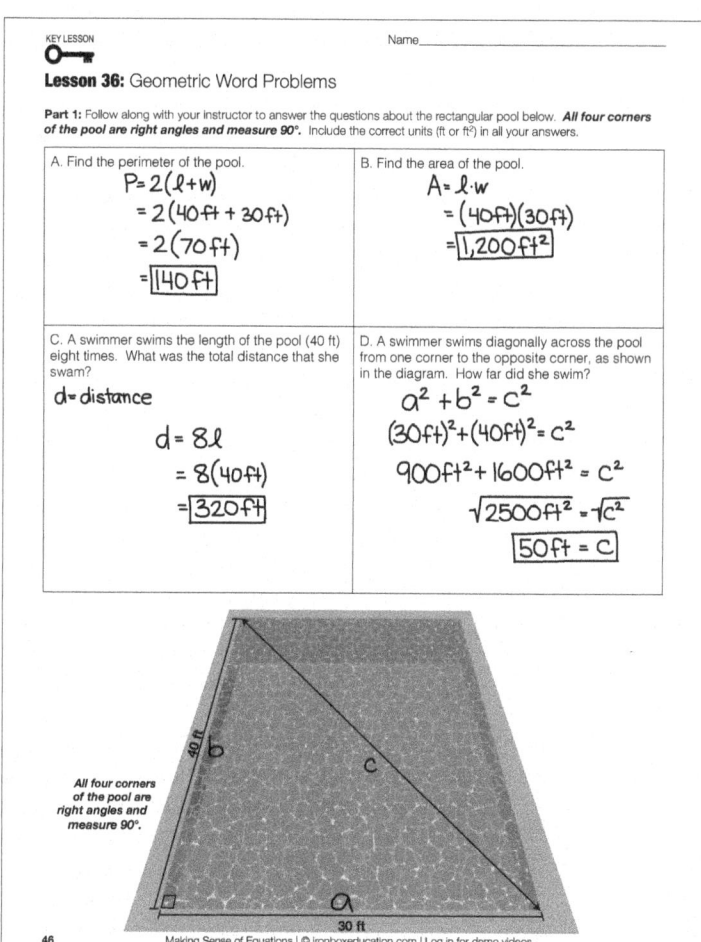

Key Points from Demo Video – Lesson 35
Perimeter and Area of Squares and Rectangles

In the previous lesson, students derived the formulas for the area and perimeter of squares and rectangles.

In Lesson 35, students practice applying these formulas.

It's important for students to <u>include the units in their calculations</u> because it will make sure they end up with the correct units in the answers.

In Box A, for example, the formula for the area of a square is $a = s^2$. Students substitute "5 mi" for s (and not just "5"), as shown below:

$A = s^2$
$= (5\text{mi})^2$

This ensures that operations that are applied to <u>numbers</u> are also applied to <u>units</u>. Both the "5" and the "mi" must be squared, giving you 25 mi².

$A = s^2$
$= (5\text{mi})^2$
$= \boxed{25\text{mi}^2}$

The correct area is 25 mi² and not 25 mi because the area in this problem is measured in square miles (mi²) and not in miles (mi).

Key Points from Demo Video – Lesson 36
Geometric Word Problems

In Lesson 36, students work with simple geometric word problems that involve area and perimeter.

Additionally, two problems involve solving problems that require knowing the length and the width of the pool.

All the word problems involve the diagram of the rectangular swimming pool.

Since the pool is rectangular, all four corners of the pool are right angles and measure 90°. This information is needed in order to use the Pythagorean Theorem in Box D.

Remember to include the correct units (ft) in the calculations. This ensures that operations that are applied to <u>numbers</u> are also applied to <u>units</u>, and it ensures that students end up with the correct unit of measurement (ft or ft²) in their answers.

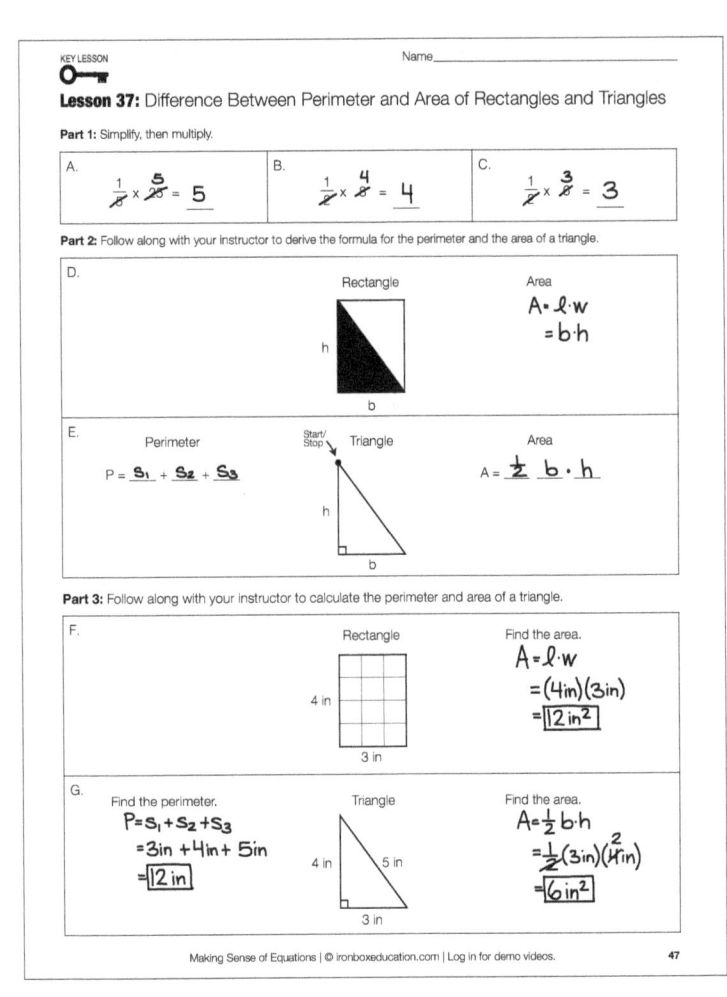

Lesson 37: Difference Between Perimeter and Area of Rectangles and Triangles

Part 1: Simplify, then multiply.

A. $\frac{1}{\cancel{5}} \times \frac{\cancel{25}^{5}}{1} = \underline{5}$

B. $\frac{1}{\cancel{2}} \times \frac{\cancel{8}^{4}}{1} = \underline{4}$

C. $\frac{1}{\cancel{2}} \times \frac{\cancel{8}^{3}}{1} = \underline{3}$

Part 2: Follow along with your instructor to derive the formula for the perimeter and the area of a triangle.

D. Rectangle — Area $A = l \cdot w = b \cdot h$

E. Perimeter $P = \underline{s_1} + \underline{s_2} + \underline{s_3}$; Triangle — Area $A = \underline{\tfrac{1}{2}} \, \underline{b} \cdot \underline{h}$

Part 3: Follow along with your instructor to calculate the perimeter and area of a triangle.

F. Rectangle — Find the area. $A = l \cdot w = (4\text{in})(3\text{in}) = \boxed{12 \text{ in}^2}$

G. Find the perimeter. $P = s_1 + s_2 + s_3 = 3\text{in} + 4\text{in} + 5\text{in} = \boxed{12 \text{ in}}$

Triangle — Find the area. $A = \tfrac{1}{2} b \cdot h = \tfrac{1}{2}(3\text{in})(4\text{in}) = \boxed{6 \text{ in}^2}$

Lesson 38: Area of Triangles (page 1 of 3)

Part 1: Find the base and the height of each triangle (use a solid line for the base and a dotted line for the height, and be sure to corner the right angle). The lengths or approximate lengths of some of the sides are provided as reference.

Right Triangles (have a right angle): 4 in, 3 in, 5 in (both triangles)

Acute Triangles (all angles < 90°): 4 in, 3 in, ~4.1 in, ~4.5 in (both triangles)

Key Points from Demo Video – Lesson 37
Difference Between Perimeter and Area of Rectangles and Triangles

In Lesson 34, students examined the differences between the perimeter and area of <u>squares</u> and <u>rectangles</u>.

In Lesson 37, students examine the differences between the perimeter and area of <u>rectangles</u> and <u>triangles</u>.

In Part 1, students practice simplifying before multiplying.

In Part 2, students follow along with their instructor to derive the formula for the perimeter and the area of a triangle, as shown in the demo video. The variable b stands for "base," and h stands for "height." Students should notice the following:

- Area of rectangle = bh
- Area of triangle = 1/2 bh

This is true because the triangle is one half of the rectangle.

In Part 3, the area of the rectangle is 12 in². The area of the triangle is one half of that, or 6 in².

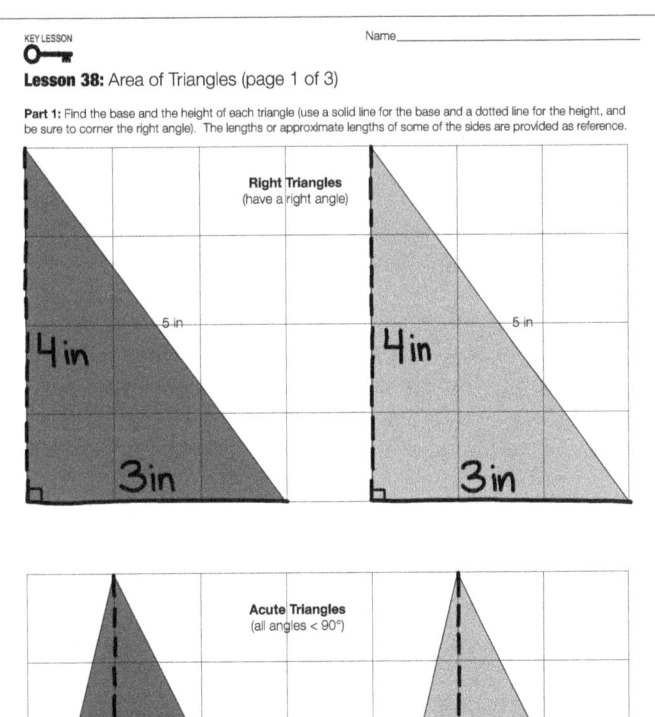

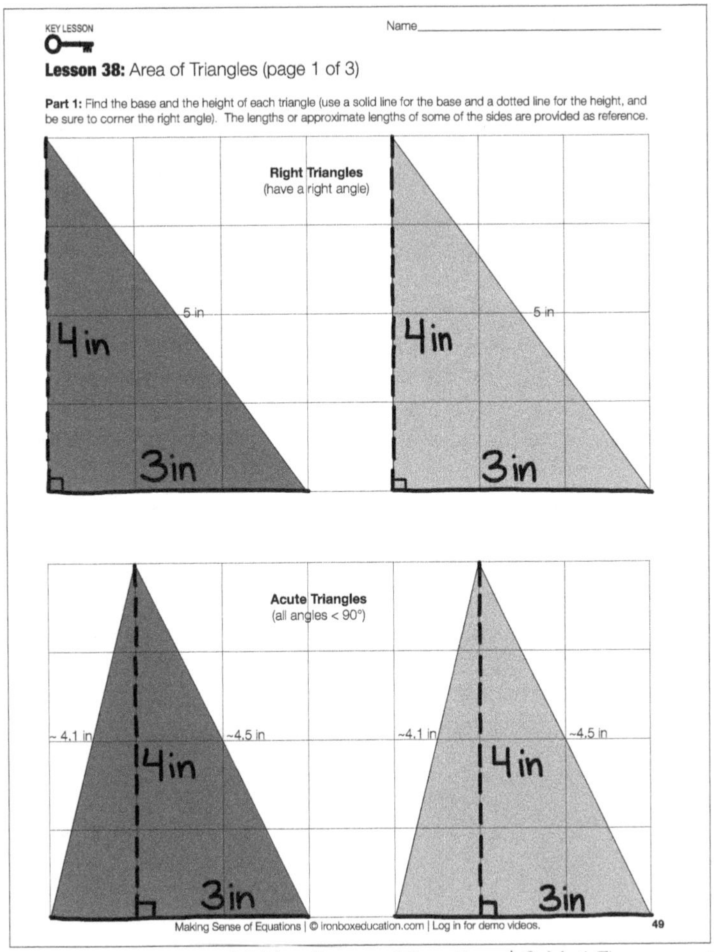

Key Points from Demo Video – Lesson 38 (page 1 of 3)
Area of Triangles

In Lesson 37, students worked with a <u>right triangle</u> and a rectangle that had the same base (3 in) and the same height (4 in). They saw that the area of the right triangle was 1/2 the area of the rectangle.

In Lesson 38, students will derive the formula for the area of <u>acute triangles</u> and <u>scalene triangles</u>.

Pages 1 and 2 of Lesson 38 have:

- a pair of right triangles (dark and light grey)
- a pair of acute triangles (dark and light)
- a pair of scalene triangles (dark and light)

Students find the base and height of each triangle.

- Use a solid line for the base (3 in).
- Use a dotted line for the height (4 in).

The height is measured from the apex of the triangle to the base. The height forms a right angle with the base. **Be sure to corner the right angle.**

(continued on the next page)

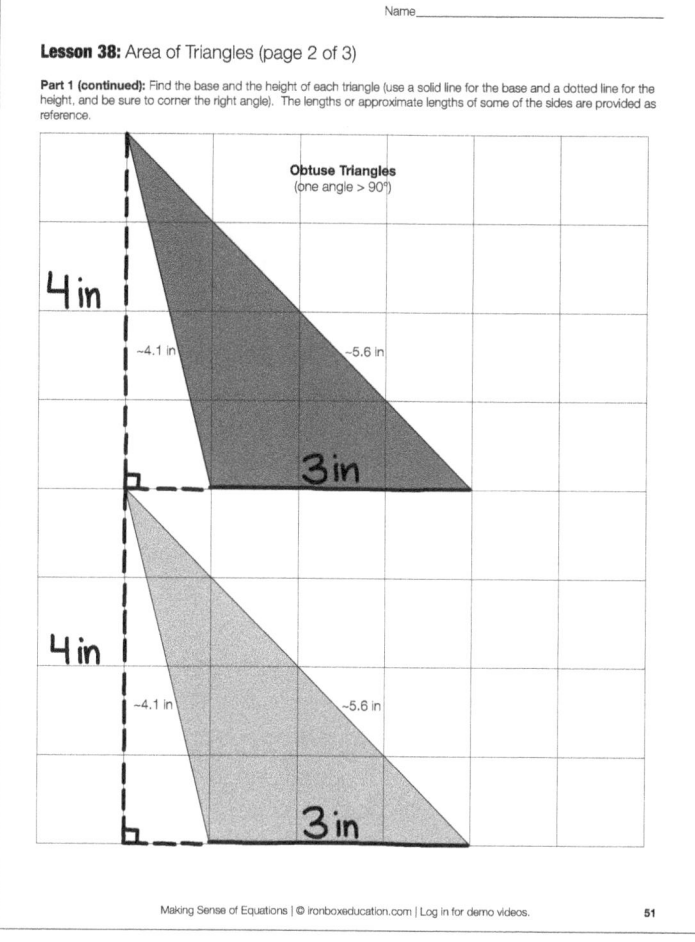

Lesson 38: Area of Triangles (page 2 of 3)

Part 1 (continued): Find the base and the height of each triangle (use a solid line for the base and a dotted line for the height, and be sure to corner the right angle). The lengths or approximate lengths of some of the sides are provided as reference.

Obtuse Triangles (one angle > 90°)

- 4 in, ~4.1 in, ~5.6 in, 3 in
- 4 in, ~4.1 in, ~5.6 in, 3 in

Key Points from Demo Video – Lesson 38 (page 2 of 3)
Area of Triangles

(continued from previous page)

The base of each obtuse triangle measures 3 in.

The height of each obtuse triangle is a little trickier to find because the height is **outside** of the figure.

Use a dotted line to extend the base line one inch to the left. To find the height, start at the apex, then draw a dotted line straight down until you reach the base.

Notice how the height forms a right angle with the base (remember to corner the angle). The height still measures 4 in, even though it is outside of the figure.

Now, students use a pair of scissors to cut out each pair of triangles.

- Keep both right triangles together.
- Keep both acute triangles together.
- Keep both obtuse triangles together.

The lesson continues on the next page.

(continued on the next page)

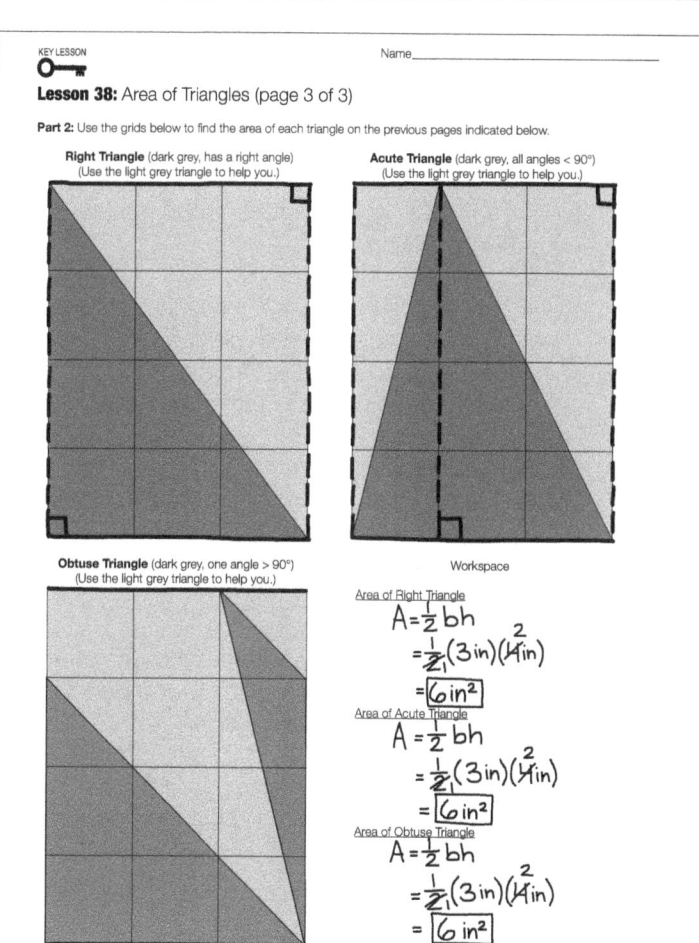

Lesson 38: Area of Triangles (page 3 of 3)

Part 2: Use the grids below to find the area of each triangle on the previous pages indicated below.

Right Triangle (dark grey, has a right angle)
(Use the light grey triangle to help you.)

Acute Triangle (dark grey, all angles < 90°)
(Use the light grey triangle to help you.)

Obtuse Triangle (dark grey, one angle > 90°)
(Use the light grey triangle to help you.)

Workspace

Area of Right Triangle
$A = \frac{1}{2}bh$
$= \frac{1}{2}(3 \text{ in})(4 \text{ in})$
$= \boxed{6 \text{ in}^2}$

Area of Acute Triangle
$A = \frac{1}{2}bh$
$= \frac{1}{2}(3 \text{ in})(4 \text{ in})$
$= \boxed{6 \text{ in}^2}$

Area of Obtuse Triangle
$A = \frac{1}{2}bh$
$= \frac{1}{2}(3 \text{ in})(4 \text{ in})$
$= \boxed{6 \text{ in}^2}$

Key Points from Demo Video – Lesson 38 (page 3 of 3)
Area of Triangles

(continued from previous page)

In this part of the lesson, students must arrange each pair of triangles and make them fit into their corresponding rectangular grids.

- Both right triangles must fit in grid #1.
- Both acute triangles must fit in grid #2.
- Both obtuse triangles must fit in grid #3.

It's very easy to fit two right triangles into the grid. Simply rotate the light grey right triangle 180°.

For the acute triangles, rotate the light grey triangle 180°, then tape the long edges together. When you try to fit the taped triangles into the grid, part of it will fall outside of the grid. **Make a single cut** along the grey triangle's height line, and move the cut-out piece over to the other side of the grid. After cutting, both acute triangles now fit perfectly into the rectangular grid.

Use similar logic for the obtuse triangles.

As shown in the demo video, the formula for the area of <u>all</u> triangles is $A = 1/2 \ bh$.

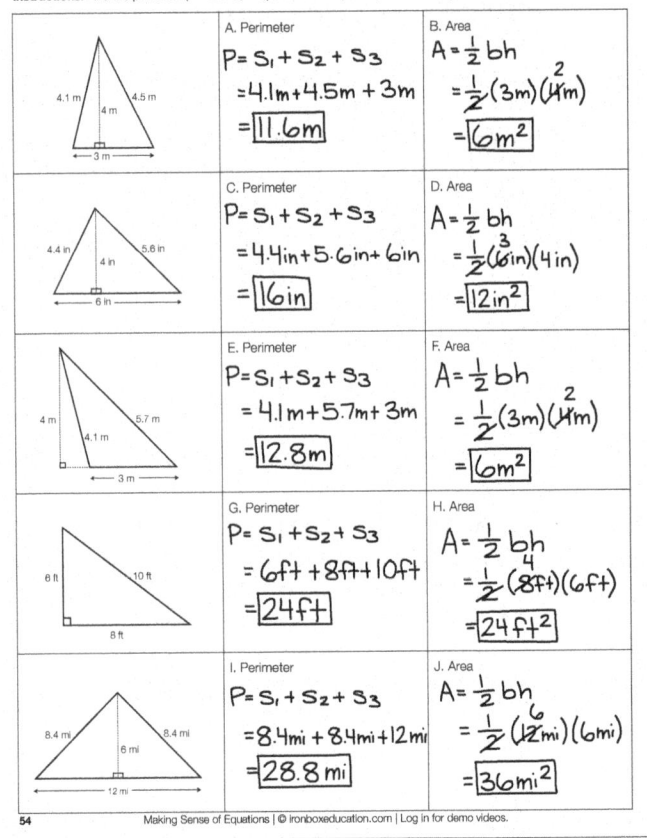

Lesson 39: Perimeter and Area of Triangles

Instructions: Find the perimeter ($P = s_1 + s_2 + s_3$) and the area ($A = bh$) of each triangle. Include the units.

Triangle	A. Perimeter	B. Area
4.1 m, 4 m, 4.5 m, 3 m	$P = s_1 + s_2 + s_3$ = 4.1m + 4.5m + 3m = **11.6m**	$A = \frac{1}{2}bh$ = $\frac{1}{2}(3m)(4m)$ = **6 m²**

	C. Perimeter	D. Area
4.4 in, 4 in, 5.6 in, 6 in	$P = s_1 + s_2 + s_3$ = 4.4in + 5.6in + 6in = **16 in**	$A = \frac{1}{2}bh$ = $\frac{1}{2}(6in)(4in)$ = **12 in²**

	E. Perimeter	F. Area
4 m, 4.1 m, 5.7 m, 3 m	$P = s_1 + s_2 + s_3$ = 4.1m + 5.7m + 3m = **12.8 m**	$A = \frac{1}{2}bh$ = $\frac{1}{2}(3m)(4m)$ = **6 m²**

	G. Perimeter	H. Area
6 ft, 10 ft, 8 ft	$P = s_1 + s_2 + s_3$ = 6ft + 8ft + 10ft = **24 ft**	$A = \frac{1}{2}bh$ = $\frac{1}{2}(8ft)(6ft)$ = **24 ft²**

	I. Perimeter	J. Area
8.4 mi, 6 mi, 8.4 mi, 12 mi	$P = s_1 + s_2 + s_3$ = 8.4mi + 8.4mi + 12mi = **28.8 mi**	$A = \frac{1}{2}bh$ = $\frac{1}{2}(12mi)(6mi)$ = **36 mi²**

KEY LESSON

Lesson 40: Pythagorean Theorem; Perimeter and Area of Triangles

Part 1: In Box A, use the Pythagorean Theorem ($a^2 + b^2 = c^2$) to find the length of the missing side. Then, use your solution from Box A to find the perimeter ($P = s_1 + s_2 + s_3$) and area ($A = 1/2 bh$).

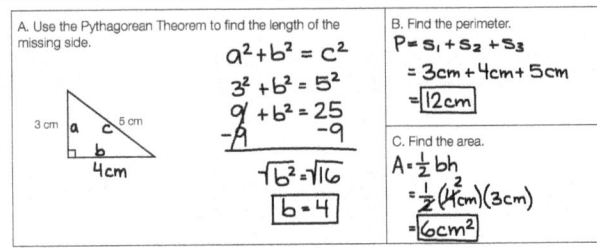

A. Use the Pythagorean Theorem to find the length of the missing side.
3 cm (a), 5 cm (c), 4 cm (b)
$a^2 + b^2 = c^2$
$3^2 + b^2 = 5^2$
$9 + b^2 = 25$
$-9 \quad -9$
$\sqrt{b^2} = \sqrt{16}$
b = 4

B. Find the perimeter.
$P = s_1 + s_2 + s_3$
= 3cm + 4cm + 5cm
= **12 cm**

C. Find the area.
$A = \frac{1}{2}bh$
= $\frac{1}{2}(4cm)(3cm)$
= **6 cm²**

Part 2: Find the length of the missing side. Then, find the perimeter and area.

D. Use the Pythagorean Theorem to find the length of the missing side.
8 m, 6 m (a), c, 10 m
$a^2 + b^2 = c^2$
$6^2 + b^2 = 10^2$
$36 + b^2 = 100$
$-36 \quad -36$
$\sqrt{b^2} = \sqrt{64}$
b = 8

E. Find the perimeter.
$P = s_1 + s_2 + s_3$
= 6m + 8m + 10m
= **24 m**

F. Find the area.
$A = \frac{1}{2}bh$
= $\frac{1}{2}(8m)(6m)$
= **24 m²**

Part 3: Find the length of the missing side. Then, find the perimeter and area.

G. Use the Pythagorean Theorem to find the length of the missing side.
5 m (a), 13 m, b, 12 m
$a^2 + b^2 = c^2$
$a^2 + 12^2 = 13^2$
$a^2 + 144 = 169$
$-144 \quad -144$
$\sqrt{a^2} = \sqrt{25}$
a = 5

H. Find the perimeter.
$P = s_1 + s_2 + s_3$
= 5m + 12m + 13m
= **30 m**

I. Find the area.
$A = \frac{1}{2}bh$
= $\frac{1}{2}(12m)(5m)$
= **30 m²**

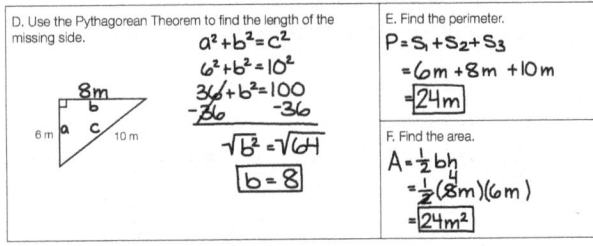

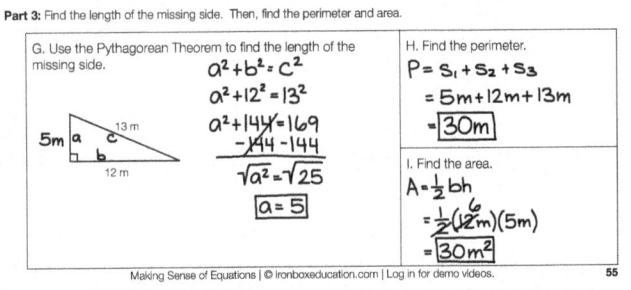

Key Points from Demo Video – Lesson 39
Perimeter and Area of Triangles

In previous lessons, students found the formulas for the area and perimeter of triangles. Additionally, they found that the formula for the area of all triangles is A = 1/2 bh.

In Lesson 39, students practice finding the perimeter and area of triangles.

The diagrams for each triangle show the length of each side. The height of each triangle is also shown. Remember, the height is perpendicular to the base (it forms a right angle with the base).

Students must use the correct measurements and the correct formulas to find the perimeter and area of each triangle.

- $P = s_1 + s_2 + s_3$
- A = 1/2 bh

Be sure to include the units in the calculations. This makes sure that the operations that are applied to numbers are also applied to units, and it makes sure that the correct units of measurement are used in the final answers. Perimeter is measured in units, and area is measured in square units.

Key Points from Demo Video – Lesson 40
Pythagorean Theorem; Perimeter and Area of Triangles

In Lesson 40, students must find the perimeter and area of each triangle, but students will not have enough information at first.

- To find the perimeter, the length of all sides is needed. One side is missing.
- To find the area, the lengths of the base and height are needed. Either the base or height is missing.

To find the missing information, students must use the Pythagorean Theorem. Then, they will have the information that they need to find the perimeter and area.

Students must be precise with this lesson. In Part 1, for example, the answers for Box B and Box C depend on the solution from Box A.

Be careful with Part 2. The triangle is flipped, and the base of the triangle is along the top edge (instead of along the bottom edge as students are accustomed to).

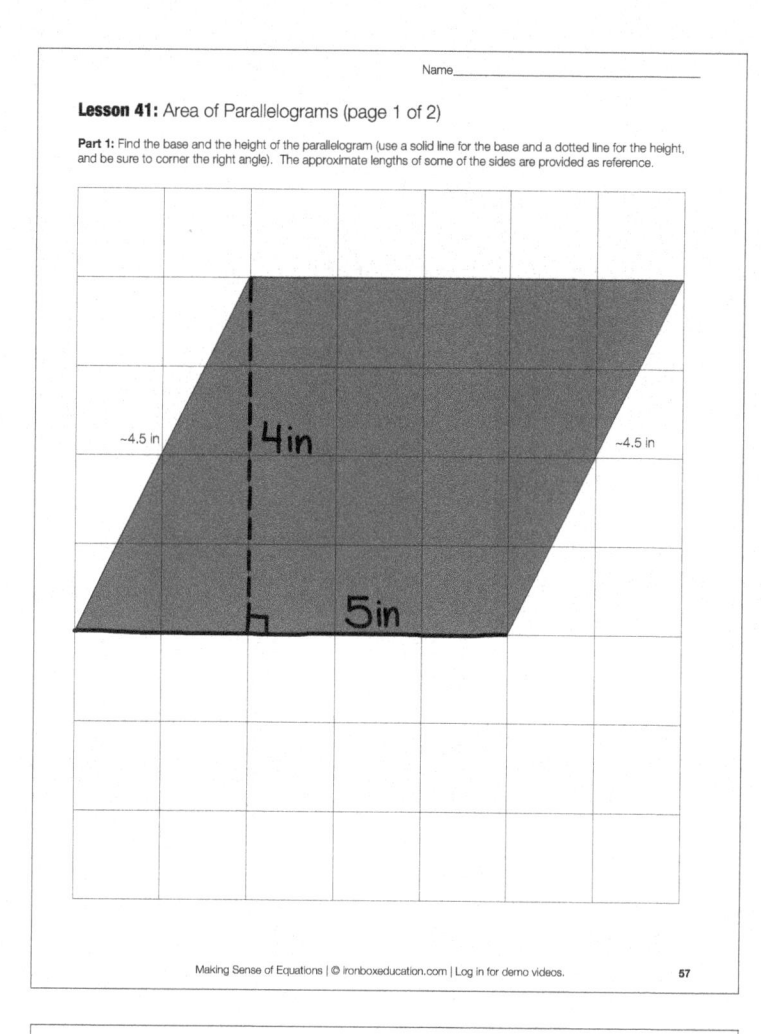

Lesson 41: Area of Parallelograms (page 1 of 2)

Part 1: Find the base and the height of the parallelogram (use a solid line for the base and a dotted line for the height, and be sure to corner the right angle). The approximate lengths of some of the sides are provided as reference.

[Parallelogram figure with ~4.5 in slanted sides, height of 4 in (dotted), and base of 5 in (solid), with right angle cornered at the base.]

Key Points from Demo Video – Lesson 41 (page 1 of 2)
Area of Parallelograms

In Lesson 38, students saw how the area of triangles and rectangles are related.

In Lesson 41, students will see how the area of parallelograms and rectangles are related.

Students find the base and height of the parallelogram.

- Use a solid line for the base.
- Use a dotted line for the height.

The height is measured from the top of the parallelogram to the base. The height forms a right angle with the base. **Be sure to corner the right angle.**

(continued on next page)

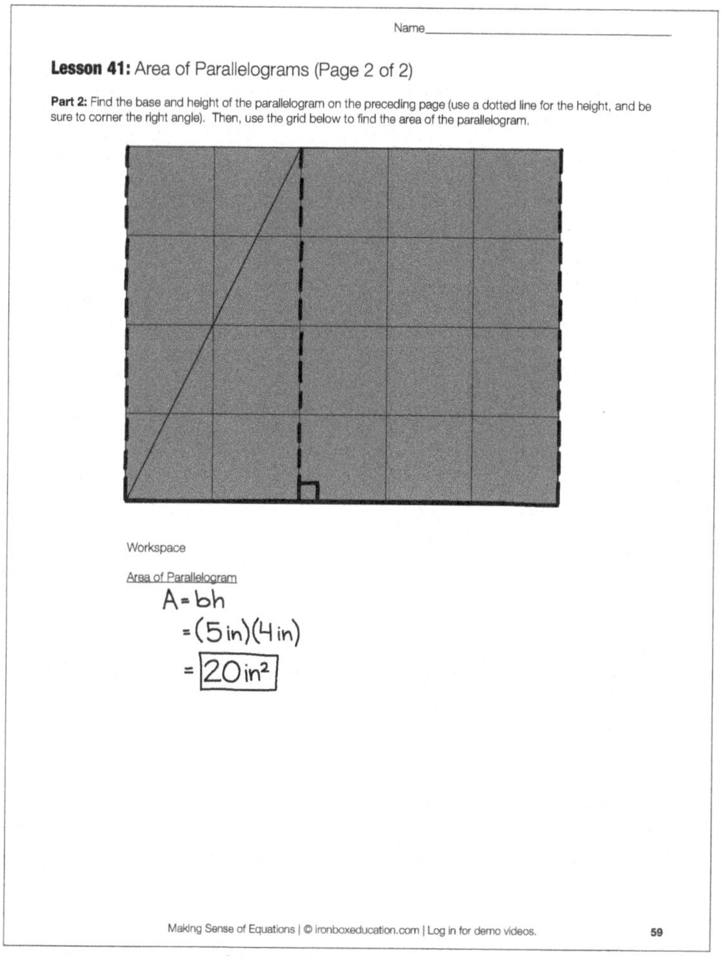

Lesson 41: Area of Parallelograms (Page 2 of 2)

Part 2: Find the base and height of the parallelogram on the preceding page (use a dotted line for the height, and be sure to corner the right angle). Then, use the grid below to find the area of the parallelogram.

Workspace

Area of Parallelogram

$A = bh$
$= (5\,in)(4\,in)$
$= \boxed{20\,in^2}$

Key Points from Demo Video – Lesson 41 (page 2 of 2)
Area of Parallelograms

(continued from previous page)

The demo video shows that in this part of the lesson, students must arrange the parallelogram and make it fit into the rectangular grid.

Part of the parallelogram will fall outside of the grid. **Make a single cut** along a height line, and move the cut-out piece over to the other side of the grid. After cutting, the parallelogram now fits perfectly into the rectangular grid.

The formula for the area of a parallelogram is:

- $A = bh$

Lesson 42: Perimeter and Area of Parallelograms

Instructions: Use the formulas $P = 2(s_1 + s_2)$ and $A = bh$ to find the perimeter and area. Include the units.

Figure	Perimeter	Area
3.6 m / 3 m / 5 m	A. Perimeter $P = 2(s_1+s_2)$ $= 2(3.6m + 5m)$ $= 2(8.6m)$ $= \boxed{17.2\,m}$	B. Area $A = bh$ $= (5m)(3m)$ $= \boxed{15\,m^2}$
3.2 ft / 3 ft / 4 ft	C. Perimeter $P = 2(s_1+s_2)$ $= 2(3.2ft + 4ft)$ $= 2(7.2ft)$ $= \boxed{14.4\,ft}$	D. Area $A = bh$ $= (4ft)(3ft)$ $= \boxed{12\,ft^2}$
8.2 in / 8 in / 8 in	E. Perimeter $P = 2(s_1+s_2)$ $= 2(8.2in + 8in)$ $= 2(16.2in)$ $= \boxed{32.4\,in}$	F. Area $A = bh$ $= (8in)(8in)$ $= \boxed{64\,in^2}$
6.4 cm / 6 cm / 4 cm	G. Perimeter $P = 2(s_1+s_2)$ $= 2(6.4cm + 4cm)$ $= 2(10.4cm)$ $= \boxed{20.8\,cm}$	H. Area $A = bh$ $= (4cm)(6cm)$ $= \boxed{24\,cm^2}$
6.7 m / 6 m / 3 m	I. Perimeter $P = 2(s_1+s_2)$ $= 2(6.7m + 3m)$ $= 2(9.7m)$ $= \boxed{19.4\,m}$	J. Area $A = bh$ $= (3m)(6m)$ $= \boxed{18\,m^2}$

Key Points from Demo Video – Lesson 42
Perimeter and Area of Parallelograms

In the previous lesson, students found the formula for the area of parallelograms.

In Lesson 42, students practice finding the perimeter and area of parallelograms.

The diagrams for each parallelogram show the length of some of the sides. The height of each parallelogram is also shown. Remember, the height is perpendicular to the base (it forms a right angle with the base).

Students must use the correct measurements and the correct formulas to find the perimeter and area of each parallelogram.

- $P = 2(s_1 + s_2)$
- $A = bh$

Be sure to include the units in the calculations. This makes sure that the operations that are applied to <u>numbers</u> are also applied to <u>units</u>, and it makes sure that the correct units of measurement are used in the final answers. Perimeter is measured in <u>units</u>, and area is measured in <u>square units</u>.

Lesson 43 is found on the next page.

Lesson 43: Area of Trapezoids (page 1 of 2)

Part 1: Find the bases and the heights of each trapezoid (use a solid line for the bases and a dotted line for the heights, and be sure to corner the right angle). The approximate lengths of some of the sides are provided as reference.

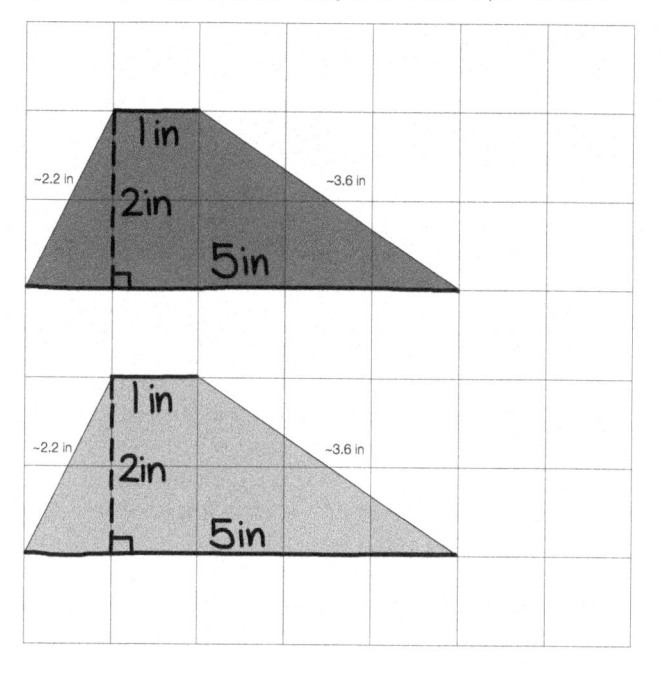

Key Points from Demo Video – Lesson 43 (page 1 of 2)
Area of Trapezoids

Lesson 38 showed that the area of <u>triangles</u> and rectangles are related.

Lesson 41 showed that the area of <u>parallelograms</u> and rectangles are related.

Lesson 43 will show that the area of <u>trapezoids</u> and rectangles are related.

Students find the lengths of both bases as well as the height of the trapezoid.

- Use a solid line for both bases.
- Use a dotted line for the height.

The height is measured from the top of the trapezoid to the base. The height forms a right angle with the base. **Be sure to corner the right angle.**

(continued on next page)

Lesson 43: Area of Trapezoids (page 2 of 2)

Part 2: Find the bases and heights of the trapezoids on the preceding page (use a dotted line for the height, and be sure to corner the right angle). Then, use the grid below to find the area of trapezoids.

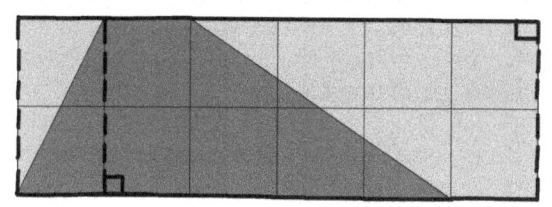

Workspace

Area of Trapezoid

$A = \frac{1}{2} h (b_1 + b_2)$

$= \frac{1}{2} (2 \text{ in})(5 \text{ in} + 1 \text{ in})$

$= \frac{1}{2} (2 \text{ in})(6 \text{ in})$

$= \boxed{6 \text{ in}^2}$

Key Points from Demo Video – Lesson 43 (page 2 of 2)
Area of Trapezoids

The demo video shows that in this part of the lesson, students must arrange both trapezoids and make them fit into the rectangular grid.

Rotate the light grey trapezoid 180°, then tape the long edges together. When you try to fit the taped trapezoids into the grid, part of it will fall outside of the grid.

Make a single cut along the light grey trapezoid's height line, and move the cut-out piece over to the other side of the grid. After cutting, both trapezoids now fit perfectly into the rectangular grid.

As shown in the demo video, the formula for the area of a trapezoid is $A = 1/2 \, h(b_1 + b_2)$.

Lesson 44: Trapezoid Equations

Part 1: Add. Use the empty white space to rewrite each problem vertically, and be sure to line up your decimal points.

A. $2.1 + 1 + 2.8 + 4 = $ **9.9**

B. $3.4 + 1 + 5.6 + 7 = $ **17**

C. $1.8 + 4.3 + 10 + 7.3 = $ **23.4**

D. $3.9 + 1 + 6 + 4 = $ **14.9**

$$\begin{array}{r}2.1\\1.0\\2.8\\+4.0\\\hline 9.9\end{array} \quad \begin{array}{r}3.4\\1.0\\5.6\\+7.0\\\hline 17.0\end{array} \quad \begin{array}{r}1.8\\4.3\\10.0\\+7.3\\\hline 23.4\end{array} \quad \begin{array}{r}3.9\\1.0\\6.0\\+4.0\\\hline 14.9\end{array}$$

Part 2: Solve. Combine like terms in the parentheses (just like "apples + apples"). Then, **simplify fractions before multiplying**. Remember to include the units in your calculations and in your answers.

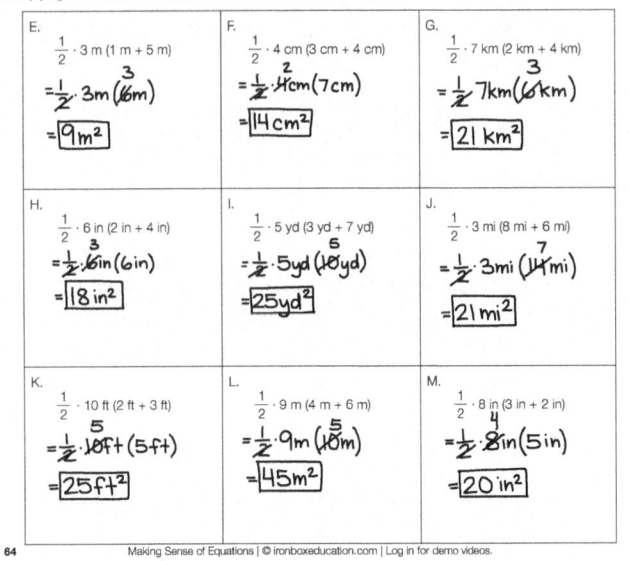

E. $\frac{1}{2} \cdot 3m (1m + 5m)$
$= \frac{1}{2} \cdot \cancel{3}m (\overset{3}{6}m)$
$= \boxed{9 m^2}$

F. $\frac{1}{2} \cdot 4cm (3cm + 4cm)$
$= \frac{1}{2} \cdot \overset{2}{\cancel{4}}cm (7cm)$
$= \boxed{14 cm^2}$

G. $\frac{1}{2} \cdot 7km (2km + 4km)$
$= \frac{1}{2} \cdot 7km (\overset{3}{\cancel{6}}km)$
$= \boxed{21 km^2}$

H. $\frac{1}{2} \cdot 6 in (2 in + 4 in)$
$= \frac{1}{2} \cdot \overset{3}{\cancel{6}}in (6in)$
$= \boxed{18 in^2}$

I. $\frac{1}{2} \cdot 5 yd (3 yd + 7 yd)$
$= \frac{1}{2} \cdot 5yd (\overset{5}{\cancel{10}}yd)$
$= \boxed{25 yd^2}$

J. $\frac{1}{2} \cdot 3 mi (8 mi + 6 mi)$
$= \frac{1}{2} \cdot 3mi (\overset{7}{\cancel{14}}mi)$
$= \boxed{21 mi^2}$

K. $\frac{1}{2} \cdot 10 ft (2 ft + 3 ft)$
$= \frac{1}{2} \cdot \overset{5}{\cancel{10}}ft (5ft)$
$= \boxed{25 ft^2}$

L. $\frac{1}{2} \cdot 9 m (4 m + 6 m)$
$= \frac{1}{2} \cdot 9m (\overset{5}{\cancel{10}}m)$
$= \boxed{45 m^2}$

M. $\frac{1}{2} \cdot 8 in (3 in + 2 in)$
$= \frac{1}{2} \cdot \overset{4}{\cancel{8}}in (5in)$
$= \boxed{20 in^2}$

Lesson 45: Perimeter and Area of Trapezoids

Instructions: Use the formulas $P = s_1 + s_2 + s_3 + s_4$ and $A = \frac{1}{2} h(b_1 + b_2)$ to find the perimeter and area.

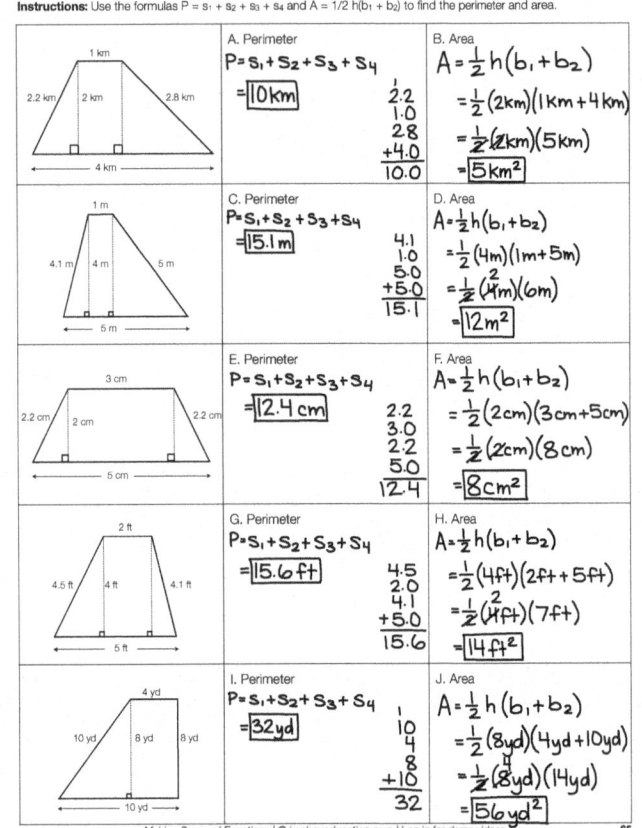

Trapezoid 1: 1 km (top), 2.2 km, 2.8 km (sides), 4 km (bottom), height 2 km

A. Perimeter
$P = s_1 + s_2 + s_3 + s_4$
$= \boxed{10 km}$
$\begin{array}{r}2.2\\1.0\\2.8\\+4.0\\\hline 10.0\end{array}$

B. Area
$A = \frac{1}{2} h (b_1 + b_2)$
$= \frac{1}{2} (2km)(1km + 4km)$
$= \frac{1}{2} (\overset{1}{\cancel{2}}km)(5km)$
$= \boxed{5 km^2}$

Trapezoid 2: 1 m (top), 4.1 m, 5 m (sides), 5 m (bottom), height 4 m

C. Perimeter
$P = s_1 + s_2 + s_3 + s_4$
$= \boxed{15.1 m}$
$\begin{array}{r}4.1\\1.0\\5.0\\+5.0\\\hline 15.1\end{array}$

D. Area
$A = \frac{1}{2} h (b_1 + b_2)$
$= \frac{1}{2} (4m)(1m + 5m)$
$= \frac{1}{2} (\overset{2}{\cancel{4}}m)(6m)$
$= \boxed{12 m^2}$

Trapezoid 3: 3 cm (top), 2.2 cm, 2.2 cm (sides), 5 cm (bottom), height 2 cm

E. Perimeter
$P = s_1 + s_2 + s_3 + s_4$
$= \boxed{12.4 cm}$
$\begin{array}{r}2.2\\3.0\\2.2\\+5.0\\\hline 12.4\end{array}$

F. Area
$A = \frac{1}{2} h (b_1 + b_2)$
$= \frac{1}{2} (2cm)(3cm + 5cm)$
$= \frac{1}{2} (\overset{1}{\cancel{2}}cm)(8cm)$
$= \boxed{8 cm^2}$

Trapezoid 4: 2 ft (top), 4.5 ft, 4.1 ft (sides), 5 ft (bottom), height 4 ft

G. Perimeter
$P = s_1 + s_2 + s_3 + s_4$
$= \boxed{15.6 ft}$
$\begin{array}{r}4.5\\2.0\\4.1\\+5.0\\\hline 15.6\end{array}$

H. Area
$A = \frac{1}{2} h (b_1 + b_2)$
$= \frac{1}{2} (4ft)(2ft + 5ft)$
$= \frac{1}{2} (\overset{2}{\cancel{4}}ft)(7ft)$
$= \boxed{14 ft^2}$

Trapezoid 5: 4 yd (top), 10 yd, 8 yd (sides), 10 yd (bottom), height 8 yd

I. Perimeter
$P = s_1 + s_2 + s_3 + s_4$
$= \boxed{32 yd}$
$\begin{array}{r}10\\4\\8\\+10\\\hline 32\end{array}$

J. Area
$A = \frac{1}{2} h (b_1 + b_2)$
$= \frac{1}{2} (8yd)(4yd + 10yd)$
$= \frac{1}{2} (8yd)(14yd)$
$= \boxed{56 yd^2}$

Key Points from Demo Video – Lesson 44
Trapezoid Equations

The formulas for the perimeter and area of trapezoids are notably more complicated than the formulas for squares, rectangles, triangles, and parallelograms.

This can cause complications when setting up and solving trapezoid equations.

Lesson 44 helps prevent these complications by building fluency in calculating the perimeter and area of trapezoids.

In Part 1, students add decimals. Use the empty white space to rewrite each problem vertically in order to line up the decimal points and place values.

In Part 2, students evaluate expressions similar to those they will see when solving trapezoid equations.

As shown in the demo video, use the order of operations, combining like terms in the parentheses (think back to the "Apples + Apples" lesson). Then, simplify fractions before multiplying.

Be sure to include the units in both the calculations and in the final answer.

Key Points from Demo Video – Lesson 45
Perimeter and Area of Trapezoids

In Lesson 43, students found the formula for the area of trapezoids. In Lesson 44, students practiced working with trapezoid expressions that have already been set up properly.

In Lesson 45, students must set up trapezoid equations themselves.

The diagrams for each trapezoid show the lengths of each side. The height of each trapezoid is also given. Remember, the height is perpendicular to the base (it forms a right angle with the base).

Students must use the correct measurements and the correct formulas to find the perimeter and area of each trapezoid.

- $P = s_1 + s_2 + s_3 + s_4$
- $A = 1/2\ h(b_1 + b_2)$

Be sure to include the units in the calculations. This makes sure that the operations that are applied to <u>numbers</u> are also applied to <u>units</u>, and it makes sure that the correct units of measurement are used in the final answers. Perimeter is measured in units, and area is measured in square units.

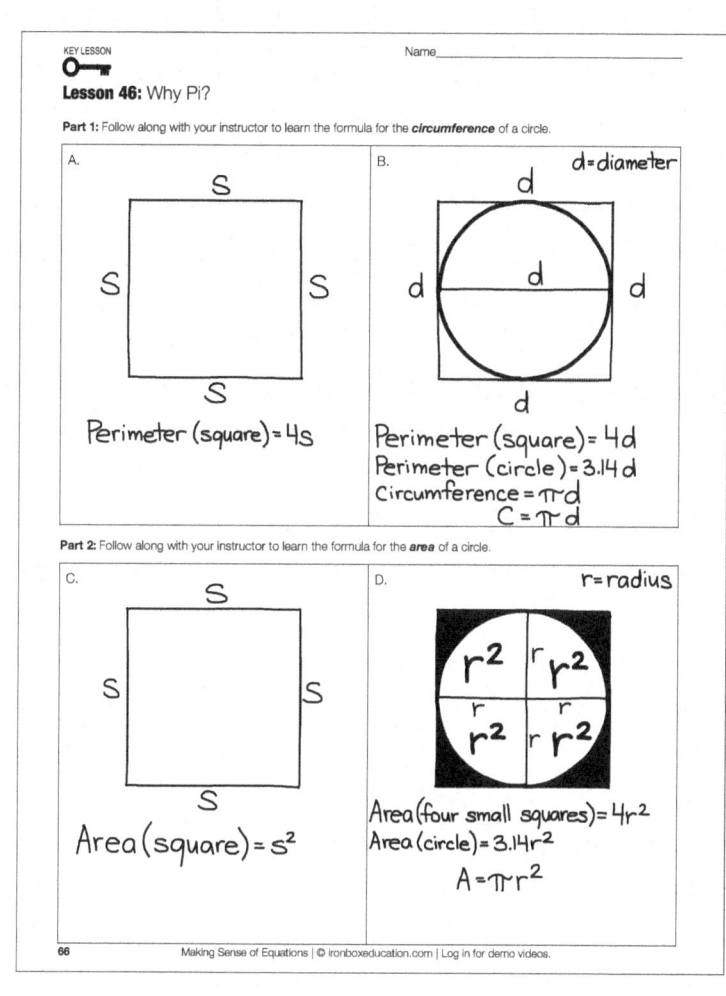

Lesson 46: Why Pi?

Part 1: Follow along with your instructor to learn the formula for the **circumference** of a circle.

A.

Perimeter (square) = 4s

B. d = diameter

Perimeter (square) = 4d
Perimeter (circle) = 3.14d
Circumference = πd
C = πd

Part 2: Follow along with your instructor to learn the formula for the **area** of a circle.

C.

Area (square) = s²

D. r = radius

Area (four small squares) = 4r²
Area (circle) = 3.14r²
A = πr²

Key Points from Demo Video – Lesson 46
Why Pi?

In previous lessons, students learned the formulas for the perimeter and area of squares, rectangles, triangles, parallelograms, and trapezoids. They also learned how the formulas for each of these figures are related to each other.

In Lesson 46, students will learn how the formulas for the perimeter and area of squares are related to the perimeter (circumference) and area of circles.

The demo video explains Parts 1 and 2 in detail.

In Box A, the perimeter of the square is 4s.

In Box B, the perimeter of the square 4d. Notice that the circle fits perfectly within the square and has the same width, but the circle is a slightly smaller shape. Likewise, the perimeter (circumference) of the circle is slightly smaller than 4d. It measures 3.14d, or πd.

In Box D, the area of each small square is r^2, so the area of the four small squares is $4r^2$. The area of the circle is slightly smaller than the area of the four small squares. Instead of measuring $4r^2$, the area of the circle measures $3.14r^2$, of $πr^2$.

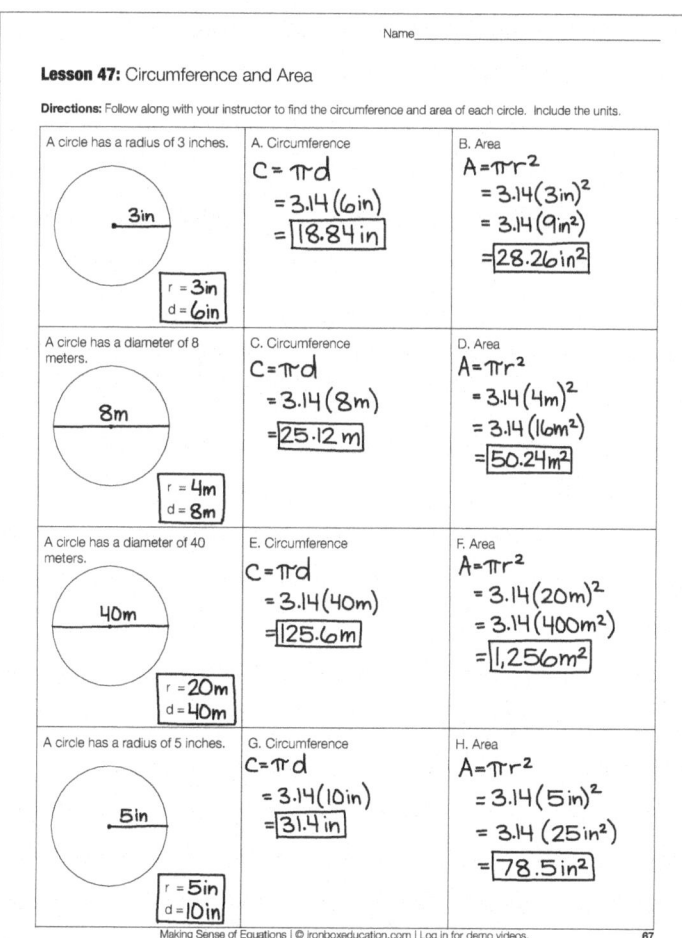

Lesson 47: Circumference and Area

Directions: Follow along with your instructor to find the circumference and area of each circle. Include the units.

A circle has a radius of 3 inches.
r = 3 in
d = 6 in

A. Circumference
C = πd
= 3.14 (6 in)
= **18.84 in**

B. Area
A = πr²
= 3.14 (3 in)²
= 3.14 (9 in²)
= **28.26 in²**

A circle has a diameter of 8 meters.
r = 4 m
d = 8 m

C. Circumference
C = πd
= 3.14 (8 m)
= **25.12 m**

D. Area
A = πr²
= 3.14 (4 m)²
= 3.14 (16 m²)
= **50.24 m²**

A circle has a diameter of 40 meters.
r = 20 m
d = 40 m

E. Circumference
C = πd
= 3.14 (40 m)
= **125.6 m**

F. Area
A = πr²
= 3.14 (20 m)²
= 3.14 (400 m²)
= **1,256 m²**

A circle has a radius of 5 inches.
r = 5 in
d = 10 in

G. Circumference
C = πd
= 3.14 (10 in)
= **31.4 in**

H. Area
A = πr²
= 3.14 (5 in)²
= 3.14 (25 in²)
= **78.5 in²**

Key Points from Demo Video – Lesson 47
Circumference and Area

In Lesson 46, students learned the formulas for the circumference and area of circles, and they learned how these formulas are related to the perimeter and area of squares.

In Lesson 47, students practice using these formulas for circles.

For each circle, students must find both the circumference and the area. This requires them to know both the diameter and radius of each circle.

However, students are given only the radius or only the diameter, but they are not given both pieces of information.

As shown in the demo video, students always figure out and write down both the radius and the diameter, even if only one of them is given in the problem.

This way, students will always have the information they need to find the circumference (C = πd) and the area (A = πr²) of circles.

Be sure to include demo units in the calculations so that you end up with the correct units in the answer.

Lesson 48: Circumference and Area (Leave Answers in Terms of π)

Directions: Find the circumference and area. Leave your answers in terms of π. Include the units.

A circle has a radius of 45 miles.
$r = 45\,mi$
$d = 90\,mi$

A. Circumference
$C = \pi d$
$= \pi(90\,mi)$
$= \boxed{90\pi\,mi}$

B. Area
$A = \pi r^2$
$= \pi(45\,mi)^2$
$= \pi(2{,}025\,mi^2)$
$= \boxed{2{,}025\pi\,mi^2}$

A circle has a diameter of 32 yards.
$r = 16\,yd$
$d = 32\,yd$

C. Circumference
$C = \pi d$
$= \pi(32\,yd)$
$= \boxed{32\pi\,yd}$

D. Area
$A = \pi r^2$
$= \pi(16\,yd)^2$
$= \pi(256\,yd^2)$
$= \boxed{256\pi\,yd^2}$

A circle has a radius of 5 inches.
$r = 5\,in$
$d = 10\,in$

E. Circumference
$C = \pi d$
$= \pi(10\,in)$
$= \boxed{10\pi\,in}$

F. Area
$A = \pi r^2$
$= \pi(5\,in)^2$
$= \pi(25\,in^2)$
$= \boxed{25\pi\,in^2}$

A circle has a radius of 65 yards.
$r = 65\,yd$
$d = 130\,yd$

G. Circumference
$C = \pi d$
$= \pi(130\,yd)$
$= \boxed{130\pi\,yd}$

H. Area
$A = \pi r^2$
$= \pi(65\,yd)^2$
$= \pi(4{,}225\,yd^2)$
$= \boxed{4{,}225\pi\,yd^2}$

Lesson 49: Volume of Cubes and Rectangular Prisms

Directions: Follow along with your instructor to complete this lesson. Find the area or volume. Include the units.

Two Dimensions (2D)

A. List the two dimensions: length, width
Name of Base shape: square
Find the area: $4\,in^2$

2 in × 2 in

$A = \ell w$ or $A = s^2$
$= (2in)(2in)$ $= (2in)^2$
$= \boxed{4\,in^2}$ $= \boxed{4\,in^2}$

C. List the two dimensions: length, width
Name of Base shape: rectangle
Find the area: $6\,in^2$

2 in × 3 in

$A = \ell w$
$= (2in)(3in)$
$= \boxed{6\,in^2}$

Three Dimensions (3D)

B. List the three dimensions: length, width, depth
Name of solid figure: cube
Find the volume: $8\,in^3$

2 in × 2 in × 2 in

$V = \ell w d$ or $V = s^3$
$= (2in)(2in)(2in)$ $= (2in)^3$
$= \boxed{8\,in^3}$ $= \boxed{8\,in^3}$

D. List the three dimensions: length, width, depth
Name of solid figure: rectangular prism
Find the volume: $12\,in^3$

2 in × 3 in × 2 in

$V = \ell w d$
$= (2in)(3in)(2in)$
$= \boxed{12\,in^3}$

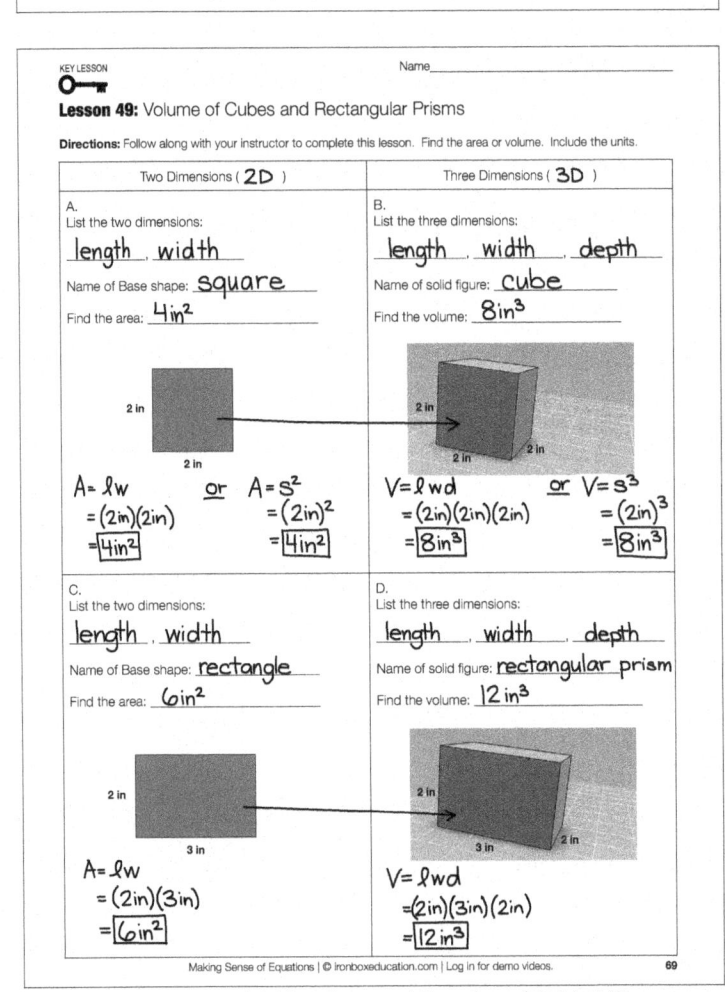

Key Points from Demo Video – Lesson 48
Circumference and Area (Leave Answers in Terms of π)

In Lesson 47, students found the circumference and area of circles.

In Lesson 48, students will again find the circumference and area of circles, but they will leave their answers in terms of π.

The reason for this is simplicity. Multiplying by π (3.14) can result in many digits and decimal places. Therefore, rather than multiplying by 3.14, we can leave our answers in terms of π (since π = 3.14).

Notice that 4,225π yd² and 13,266.5 yd² are equivalent, but 4,225π yd² is simpler.

As shown in the demo video, students always figure out and write down both the radius and the diameter, even if only one of them is given in the problem.

This way, students will have all the information they need to find the circumference (C = πd) and the area (A = πr²) of circles.

Be sure to include the units in the calculations so that you end up with the correct units in the answer.

Key Points from Demo Video – Lesson 49
Volume of Cubes and Rectangular Prisms

In previous lessons, students learned how the equations for various geometric figures are related.

In Lesson 49, students will learn the following:

- The equations for the <u>area of squares</u> and the <u>volume of cubes</u> are related.
- The equations for the <u>area of rectangles</u> and the <u>volume of rectangular prisms</u> are related.

Box A and Box B compare squares and cubes.

- The area of the square is measured using two dimensions (2D) – length and width.
- The volume of the cube is measured using three dimensions (3D) – length, width, and depth. Notice that a cube resembles a square with depth.

Box C and Box D compare rectangles and rectangular prisms.

- The area of the rectangle is measured in 2D.
- The volume of the rectangular prism is measured in 3D. Notice that a rectangular prism resembles a rectangle with depth.

Lesson 50: Volume of Cubes and Rectangular Prisms

Directions: Name each solid figure. Then, find the volume. Remember to include the units in both your calculations and in your answer. Use **length**, **width**, and **height** as your three dimensions.

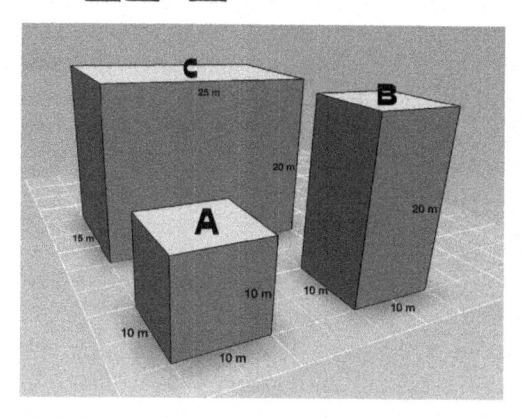

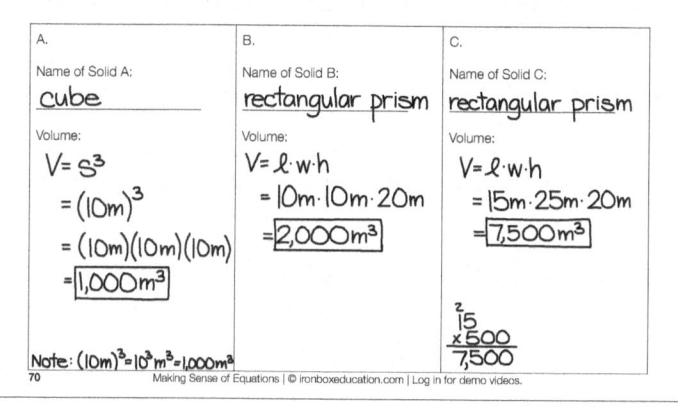

[Figure: Three solids labeled A (cube, 10m × 10m × 10m), B (rectangular prism, 10m × 10m × 20m), and C (rectangular prism, 15m × 25m × 20m)]

A.
Name of Solid A: cube
Volume:
$V = s^3$
$= (10m)^3$
$= (10m)(10m)(10m)$
$= \boxed{1,000 m^3}$

Note: $(10m)^3 = 10^3 m^3 = 1,000 m^3$

B.
Name of Solid B: rectangular prism
Volume:
$V = \ell \cdot w \cdot h$
$= 10m \cdot 10m \cdot 20m$
$= \boxed{2,000 m^3}$

C.
Name of Solid C: rectangular prism
Volume:
$V = \ell \cdot w \cdot h$
$= 15m \cdot 25m \cdot 20m$
$= \boxed{7,500 m^3}$

$\begin{array}{r} \overset{2}{15} \\ \times 500 \\ \hline 7,500 \end{array}$

Key Points from Demo Video – Lesson 50
Volume of Cubes and Rectangular Prisms

In Lesson 49, students learned the formulas for the volume of a cube and the volume of a rectangular prism.

In Lesson 50, students practice applying these formulas.

There is one important difference in this lesson. Instead of using length, width, and <u>depth</u> as the three dimensions, use length, width, and **height.**

In Box A, the formula for the volume of a cube is $V = s^3$.

In Box B and Box C, the formula for the volume of a rectangular prism is $V = \ell \cdot w \cdot h$.

Include the units in the calculations to make sure that operations that are applied to numbers are also applied to units.

In Box A, for example, the volume of the cube is $(10m)^3$. The "10" and the "meters" must both be cubed. This gives you 1,000 m³, or 1,000 cubic meters. This is correct since volume is measure in cubic units.

Lesson 51: Volume of Triangular Prisms

Directions: Follow along with your instructor to complete this lesson. Find the area or volume.

Two Dimensions (2D)	Three Dimensions (3D)
A. List the two dimensions: length (base), height Name of Base shape: triangle Find the area: 3 ft² [triangle: 3 ft base, 2 ft height] $A = \frac{1}{2} bh$ $= \frac{1}{2}(3ft)(2ft)$ $= \boxed{3 ft^2}$	**B.** List the three dimensions: length (base), height, depth Name of solid figure: triangular prism Find the volume: 15 ft³ [triangular prism: 3 ft, 2 ft, 5 ft] $V = \frac{1}{2} bhd$ $= \frac{1}{2}(3ft)(2ft)(5ft)$ $= \boxed{15 ft^3}$
C. List the two dimensions: length (base), height Name of Base shape: triangle Find the area: 12 m² [triangle: 6 m base, 4 m height] $A = \frac{1}{2} bh$ $= \frac{1}{2}(6m)(4m)$ $= \boxed{12 m^2}$	**D.** List the three dimensions: length (base), height, depth Name of solid figure: triangular prism Find the volume: 84 m³ [triangular prism: 6 m, 4 m, 7 m] $V = \frac{1}{2} bhd$ $= \frac{1}{2}(6m)(4m)(7m)$ $= \boxed{84 m^3}$

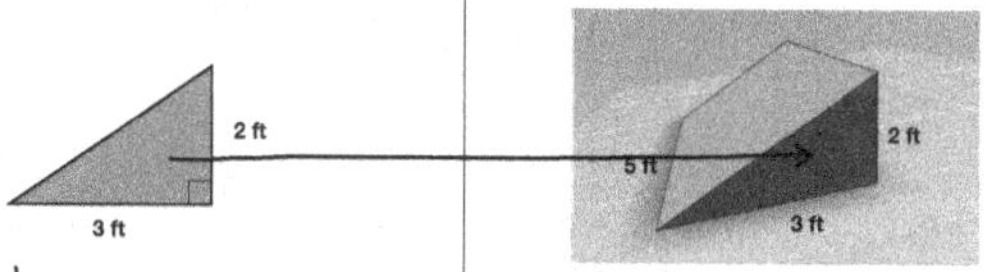

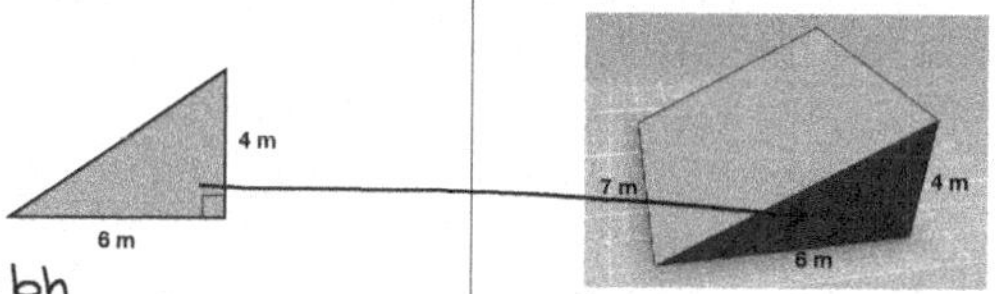

Key Points from Demo Video – Lesson 51
Volume of Triangular Prisms

In Lesson 49, students learned the following:

- The equations for the <u>area of squares</u> and the <u>volume of cubes</u> are related.
- The equations for the <u>area of rectangles</u> and the <u>volume of rectangular prisms</u> are related.

In Lesson 51, students will learn the following:

- The equations for the <u>area of triangles</u> and the <u>volume of triangular prisms</u> are related.

Box A and Box B compare a triangle with a triangular prism.

- The area of the triangle is measured using two dimensions – length (base) and height.
- The volume of the triangular is measured using three dimensions (3D) – length (base), height, and depth. Notice that a triangular prism resembles a triangle with depth.

Include the units in both the calculations and in the final answer. Area is measured in <u>square units</u>, and volume is measured in <u>cubic units</u>.

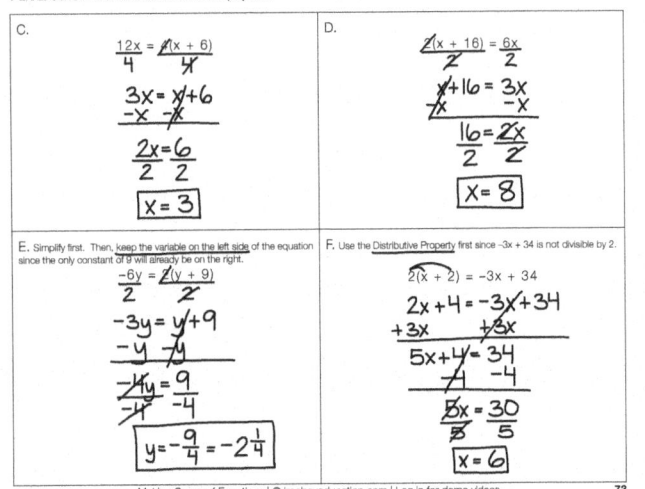

Key Points from Demo Video – Lesson 52
Variables on Both Sides of the Equation

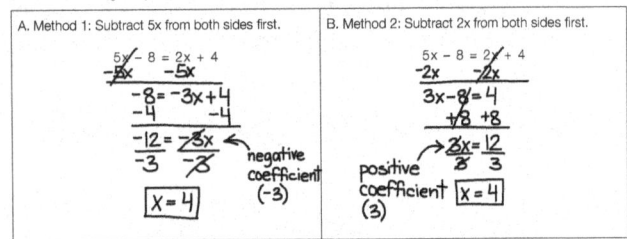

In Lesson 52, students work with equations that have variables on both sides of the equation. Students should get the variable on one side of the equation (either the left side or the right side), and they should get the constant on the other side of the equation.

In Part 1, students follow along with their instructor to learn two ways of the solving the same equation. The equation is $5x - 8 = 2x + 4$.

In Box A (Method 1), students first subtract 5x from both sides of the equation. This will result in the equation $-8 = -3x + 4$, which has a negative coefficient (–3) in front of the variable (x).

In Box B (Method 2), students first subtract 2x from both sides of the equation. This will result in the equation $3x - 8 = 4$, which has a positive coefficient (3) in front of the variable (x).

In Part 2, students solve each equation. The hint says, "Stay positive." Students need to decide whether to move the variables to either the left side or the right side of the equation. For these problems, choose the side that keeps the coefficients positive.

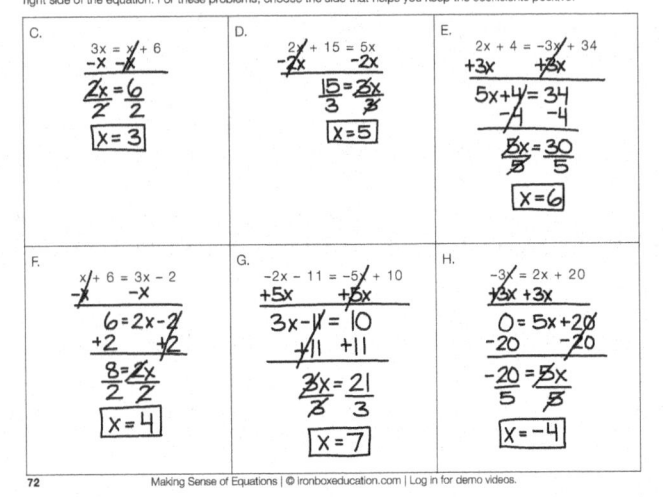

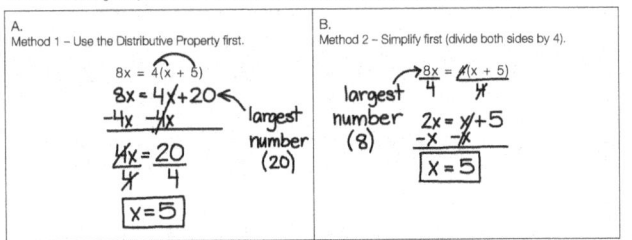

Key Points from Demo Video – Lesson 53
Variables on Both Sides of the Equation

In Lesson 53, students continue working with equations that have variables on both sides of the equation.

In Part 1, students follow along with their instructor to learn two ways of the solving the same equation. The equation is $8x = 4(x + 5)$.

In Box A (Method 1), students use the Distributive Property first. This will result in the equation $8x = 4x + 20$.

In Box B (Method 2), students simplify first by dividing both sides of the equation by 4. This results in the equation $2x = x + 5$.

Notice that by using Method 2 (simplify first instead of using the Distributive Property first), you avoid having to work with larger numbers. The largest number in Method 1 was 20, and the largest number in Method 2 was 8.

In Part 2, students solve each equation. Students should simplify first unless otherwise directed.

Lesson 54: Multi-Step Equations

Part 1: Follow along with your instructor to solve each equation.

A.
$72 = 6x + 3x$
$\frac{72}{9} = \frac{9x}{9}$
$\boxed{x = 8}$

B.
$3x + 5x - 2 = 54$
$8x - 2 = 54$
$ +2 +2$
$\frac{8x}{8} = \frac{56}{8}$
$\boxed{x = 7}$

C.
$11x - 2x + 4 = 10$
$9x + 4 = 10$
$ -4 -4$
$\frac{9x}{9} = \frac{6}{9}$
$x = \frac{6}{9}$
$\boxed{x = \frac{2}{3}}$

D. Use the Distributive Property first.
$11 = -4(-6x - 3)$
$11 = 24x + 12$
$-12 -12$
$\frac{-1}{24} = \frac{24x}{24}$
$\boxed{x = -\frac{1}{24}}$

E. Solve by inspection.
$\frac{3}{-7(40-5)} = \frac{x}{-7(40-5)}$
$\boxed{x = 3}$

F. Solve by inspection.
$-6 = -(x + 4)$
$\boxed{x = 2}$

G.
$\cancel{5} \cdot \frac{8x-1}{\cancel{5}} = 5 \cdot 3$
$8x - 1 = 15$
$ +1 +1$
$\frac{8x}{8} = \frac{16}{8}$
$\boxed{x = 2}$

H.
$\cancel{2} \cdot \frac{3x-1}{\cancel{2}} = (x+3)2$
$3x - 1 = 2x + 6$
$-2x -2x$
$x - 1 = 6$
$ +1 +1$
$\boxed{x = 7}$

I.
$5(-6) = \frac{4x+6}{\cancel{5}} \cancel{5}$
$-30 = 4x + 6$
$-6 -6$
$\frac{-36}{4} = \frac{4x}{4}$
$\boxed{x = -9}$

J. LCM = 8
$8\left(\frac{1}{8}x + \frac{1}{4}\right) = (2)8$
$x + 2 = 16$
$ -2 -2$
$\boxed{x = 14}$

K. LCM = 9
$9\left(\frac{1}{9}x + \frac{1}{3}\right) = \left(\frac{2}{\cancel{3}}\right)\cancel{9}^{3}$
$x + 3 = 6$
$ -3 -3$
$\boxed{x = 3}$

L. LCM = 2
$2\left(\frac{1}{2}x\right) = (2x - 12)2$
$x = 4x - 24$
$-4x -4x$
$\frac{-3x}{-3} = \frac{-24}{-3}$
$\boxed{x = 8}$

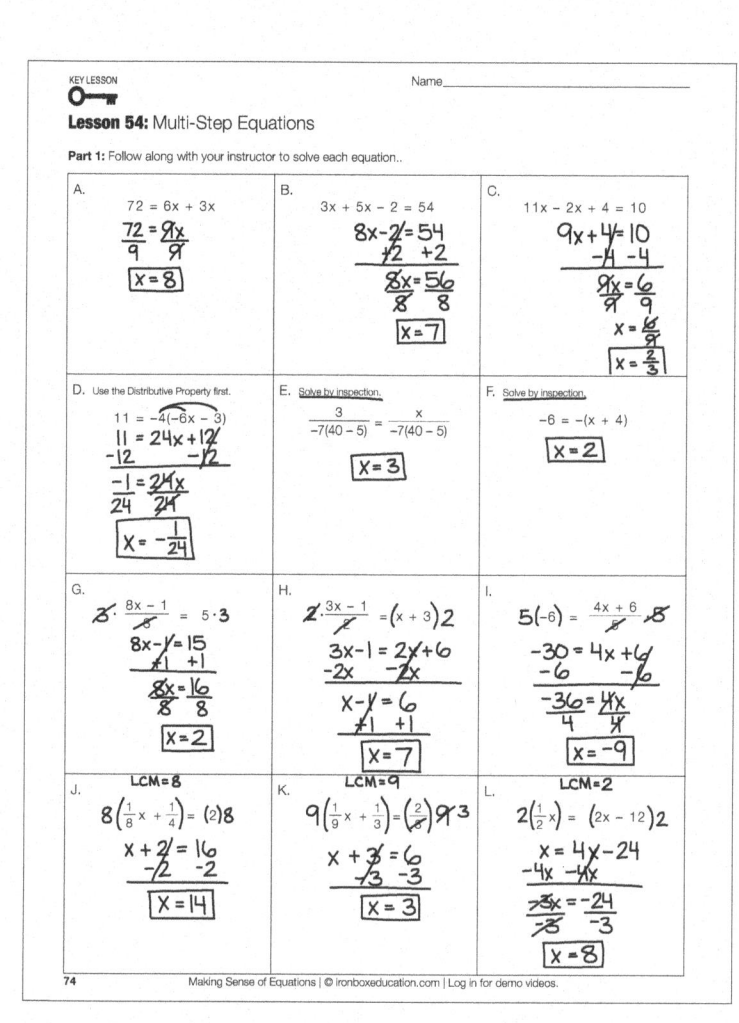

Key Points from Demo Video – Lesson 54
Multi-Step Equations

In Lesson 54, students follow along with their instructor to solve multi-step equations. All three problems in each row are similar problems.

In Row 1 (Boxes A-C), the first step involves combining like terms. In Box A, for example, the first step is to add 6x and 3x to give you 9x. This is just like adding "apples plus apples" from the book *Making Sense of Fractions.*

In Row 2 (Boxes D-F), each problem involves the Distributive Property. Boxes E and F, however, should be solved by inspection and by not actually working out the entire problem. As shown in the demo video, it's easy to use a shortcut in Boxes E and F, and you can see the answers at a glance.

In Row 3 (Boxes G-I), multiply by the reciprocal to simplify the fraction on one side of the equation.

In Row 4 (Boxes J-L), multiply both sides of equation by the LCM of the fractions in order to simplify the equations.